A Dragonhoard Of Pigeons

poems by Dave Medd

Published in 2025 by FeedARead Publishing

British Library C.I.P.

A CIP catalogue record for this title is available from the British Library

Magic Ink

I'll mail you
a clean sheet of paper.

Wear it,
this winter,
over your heart.

See how
the poems
appear.

Acknowledgements

Some of these poems have been published in *Outposts Poetry Quarterly, Orbis, Dream Catcher, The Coffee House, Obsessed With Pipework, The Cicerone Journal, Blue River Review, Otherwise Engaged, Alchemy Spoon, Dreich, The Morning Star,* and on *I Am Not A Silent Poet*

Front cover photo: Hull Fair, 2022

Back cover photo: Traditional Lithuanian musicians welcome the travellers

Contents

Amateurs

Curtain rises on her last performance,
one week in a north-east coast resort
    church hall, tail ending summer.
Overture done. Final beginning in full swing,
first chorus winging their way through wedding revels,
        bridesmaiding laughter.

Our glum guest harbours dark imagination,
gumboot characters weave an unreal pageant,
    sweet-selling harvest and fire.
But oh! Just look at the dancers! Look at the girls!
Here is a world worth waiting a holiday for.
        Walloping theatre!

And moments won from madness gild the debris.
Spent squibs of our season on the turn
    scurry moonwise and dwindle.
Look at that dancer there. Bright eyes and dimples
punctuate our farce with rhyme and tears,
        leavening winter.

So go now, catch in your palm her falling star.
Dazzle, dead Jack walking, as her gold heel
    spins in the hall of your verses.
She is the land and sea and the dark dancing.
See how the guy in her bone fire capers and sings,
          dances with jangles.

Finding Dylan Thomas

In 1965, I discovered folk music,
Bob Dylan and Dylan Thomas, in that order.
Old school notes, receipts, newspaper cuttings,
Bell Punch tickets bussed from sixties' journeys –

the book still reads my finger stains, gives up
raw teenage whispers, rakish ghouls.
Pages thick, worth holding, finger and thumb
turning, pause, taste, laying to rest.

Hot-wrought, black print shapes word enough to roll,
gobstopper, on your tongue. Change colour with spit.
Or swim with your sockets' fuse, moist for a glance,
to dance, with foxes, down a moment's labyrinth.

Eighteen, original lovers wrinkle now,
crinkle-rough-cut, diamond edges stained,
fogged, smelling of dawn-bed dew and cool,
on lips and lots I thought I knew.

Light Stains

This that I make for you must be
a strange bird in the magnolia tree,
a stain of light on frosted panes,
a breaking rose in autumn rain.
This empty vase on the window sill
is a tale too long, too cold to tell;
glass of wine in December snow,
a line, a leaf, a letter's glow
on the mat when nobody heard the knock
of the post, or the ghost of a step on the track.

This pattern of whispers under the lens
teams mad with stars that prick like whins;
turn of dreams, this ravel of cares
unwinds like a curl of hair on the stairs
or twist of ribbon, wrap of a scarf;
print of winter's wish on the hearth,
faintest trace of ash from fire
burning as long as, as long as forever.

Haunting Places

Wet with breath of being here,
schools, with infant stages, open
sky-blue curtains through their wild
proscenium. Corners harbour milk-crate,

monkey towers, iron-cold
for climbing. Corridors reek morning
sawdust, soaked in disinfectant's
anxious rain, recalling war.

Shops infuse with movie-scented
soap, mingling grocer spells
of hope. Cold meat hums by the singing
slicer. Scouring powders fizz,

in kaleidoscope tubes, exploding memory
under the kitchen sink. Butter
blocks out pat. Phosphors and sulphurs,
floor cloth and matches, retail broken

biscuits in assortment, urchin
tins. Damp church, old wood crawls
with hassocks and wax. Our haunting places,
shadows and crevices, are where we linger,

touching the arm of someone's lover's
memory ghost. Brick and stone
remember rain and sunlight, damp
with droplets of our passing. Fingered

wood records, in glyphs and runes,
our passion chatter, glottal stains
and clicks. This text remains,
our heartbeats in the rafters.

Baked Hedgehog

Twenty stone of monolith, whopping barrel-belly,
they called him Durham Bob in Seaton Sluice.
Grey jowls, saggy sacks that shook in scowls and quarrels;
round as an o, scarified, sculleried face;
eye pin sapphires; hair like frost skeins;
a name to craft alien status north of the Tyne.

Sang as a boy in his cathedral choir
(better at whistling now in the club's hot fume,
driving comrades mad with impish joy).
Brown paper under his vest kept winters warm,
a parcel of wheezes. Bragged like an old myth's bear,
steeling apprentices with a fistful of roar.

He could quote the rule book line for line, bonny lad,
keep committee secretaries straight;
lit seam and shaft with language and lamp.
Once, when snow was mindless, turning white
all hope of work, trudged four miles, to keep
the pit wheel grinding up tradition's heap.

Should have drunk less; beer flushed out his dreams.
They found him once, near death, in long dune grass,
collapsed, a savage comedy of forms.
Fancied girls and pigeons by the gross.
Indefensible. Unreconstructed. Didn't
hold with bloody swearing in front of women.

Pit crippled arm he cradled like a sick child to his heart.
Needed a hand with his coat, and that was a privilege
of sorts. Grey sea niggled through the cut
and washed old bottles from the fisher's vantage.
He declared best Yorkshire puddings need pigeons' eggs;
best poacher, knew the best butcher; he could bake hedgehogs.

A Song Of The Bath

Do you remember the bath, my bonny?
    Do you remember steam?
Do you remember live coals in the fire,
    flickering figures of dream?
Do you remember the tap in the yard,
    water dribbling ice?
Dark, winter nights she would carry the pans
    to the copper, light the blue gas.

Do you remember the Palm Court Hotel
    and the valley of Lorna Doone?
The wireless, crackling up on a shelf,
    to a dad-and-them, sad-again tune?
Lapped in bright water, before the black grate,
    her watching chair rocked and creaked,
so much to carry, to fire, to pour –
    small wonder it chanced once a week.

Remember we stood up, heads bowed, in the dark,
    remember we knew all the words?
Knew how to fasten hope to a nightmare,
    owned sets of cigarette cards?
Remember the pedigree, blackout and Goons,
    sirens they tested, in case?
Postcards and strange, tarnished medals, unworn,
    in a box, in a dark secret place?

Remember those bath nights in front of the fire,
    just six or eight times, no more.
Second baptism, no vicar, no choir,
    just drips on the clippy mat floor?
And do we remember the showers and baths,
    many thousands we've taken since then?
Do we hell! Just fire and water, my bonny,
    anthems we'll not sing again.

Old Selves

Sifting through songs in a box in the attic,
    I came across one I'd forgotten,
looped and festooned with a scramble of green,
    tumbling out of the quarry.
Poultice of undergrowth, earth and shine,
    sharpness of nettle hair,
with flowers hung like sea-worm eggs
    in the mould of the morning air,
and lipstick-smeared willow herb,
    like the long fly's pupa,
hosting a ghost of whispers and flares,
    the faded parade of a trooper.

For years, I believed, at the back of it all,
    I found a magnolia tree,
alien, unexpected, lost,
    locked in a strange ravine.
A white queen, mired in city loam,
    back to the cold rock wall,
swayed and danced her numerous arms,
    magic and ivory pearls,
blossom, naked as hares on a mountain,
    luminous silk in the mist,
lifting and blessing and tracing an ancient
    pedigree older than bees.

Now, here am I, out on a pauper stage,
    singing for kids for a crust.
Suddenly, next to me, patched up in murmurs,
    dappled in patterns of rust,
my fingers on strings cracking knuckles like walnuts,
    you, leaning your head on my shoulder,
dancing in time to the wind of the rhyme,
    your hair in my neck like a spider.
Heavy with damp and the moon on my sleeve,
    I can smell meadowsweet,
though I'm back in my attic, where all the old selves
    flock to their roots in the peat.

Laburnum

Barefoot terrace in starveling splendour -
little to commend it nowadays.
Ragtag barbarian, chimney banter,
moon sellers, dream weavers, beggars and strays
lintel and sill-spuggy grandstand,
bays hallow ferns and marble washstands.
Old girls hope for a bandstand
hot-full of boys who take their rugby neat,
meanwhile, the yard out back is breaking light.

Lived here once, midwinter hearth,
halfway haunt, easy time
safe-house lodged in mission garth,
midway this pilgrim pantomime.
Living room weather-bound,
a bug infested willow leaned,
blocked light the window round.
Caliban of the flatlands filled our heads
with shadow flies and rumour of old gods.

Meanwhile, shackled and cramped at the back,
a laburnum slumped on an iron gate.
Lean god landed, humptied, cracked,
thin trunk twisted, all but snapped,
dodging the gaze of voyeur and looter,
harbouring jewels of hoofer and bleater,
travelling poet and player.
Vagrant mongrels fouled promethean seed
with a dollop of crap. Sniff and lick. Check out the breed.

Northern twilight soon runs cold.
Neighbour's cat savours flame on her tongue
and the wedding guest leaves gold gifts
on a carpet of fire. Shiver and sing.
The lane witch peddles yellow thimbles,
warding off sleep by nips and numbers.
The night wind stirs her embers.
Time to leave, before the word breaks fire
or midas pods drop from my lips like flowers.

On Field

There was this field, wilderness,
city's edge, a land undressed
where children might get lost.
Skylark commandoes trained in boy-high grass
and, hot in hollows, shedding skins like jumpers,
girls drew down a moon to ride the moss.
Their barley hair pooled plain and heap.
Nettle and thorn in flood, come winter
bleak, froze flat like steppe.

There was this hole. We made it legend,
called it our bomb hole. We could pretend
to find shrill bits of our bomb.
Unexploded shards of a vagrant dream,
under a thorn bush, locked in a lair, a hint,
days before we came that didn't count,
triggered a wasting sickness, rained
hot summer scent, forbidden dews
to leave our white limbs stained.

They made this park, a sterile pool,
white and clean and chlorine cool.
Roundabouts to catch the sun
before he knew a summer's itch;
frames for iron monkeys to be kings,
and a grand old swing, tumbled up, or down in a ditch;
a slide for sweeping under the grave
to ground, to festering under the skin.
The bloody land felt safe.

Wilderness deep as maggot's dark,
frozen girls awoke at back
of dump, to button cardigans,
smooth crushed grass and hot, red dust from gingham
blue-bright skirts. Oh yes, we bring and carry
fragments of our bomb. Now, locked in a dug-out,
the old moon in her folly
lies restless in my arms, picking hawthorn
shrapnel from her belly.

First Song Of The Clown

Clown is painting his face on a massive
egg from Africa. Two small holes,
where plasm of bird was blown like smoke,
    let in the circus gales.
What ought to be empty is stuffed with souls
of comic one liners, gags in the dark,
shaggy dog stories let off the leash,
    wagging their tails in the park.
And inside this replica, memory shards
fall open, like fragile Valentine cards.

Polish perfect, white as a fridge,
black diamond eyes, mined by the crack
and collapse of a million laughter tons
    on Clown's imperfect back.
His mouth is red as a rhododendron
gashed on Spring-green earth and rocks;
changed face, like the jacket of Alice's guardsman,
    locked in a wardrobe box.
High on a wire, a dancing lady
pirouettes on vanishing glory.

Come morning, the painted grin is wide
as a fallow field. And now the circus dims.
All gallopers reined to a gasp and stop
    and clop. The stilt man shrinks
to a bank clerk. Lion follows his pride.
The tightrope lady, down on her luck,
folds herself painfully back inside
    the verses of his book.
Clown, with an icicle, carves one more blotch
on the shell of his face, in the tinder box.

A Rhyme From The Nursery

With the Jack of Spades and Jonah
playing poker on the deck,
radio belting opera,
ship a total wreck,
who knows how the time blows, now
there's none aboard to check?

Sandman and his lantern left
long fairytales ago.
Snowman lost his buttons,
dark began to flow.
Guy leapt from his bonfire,
once the bones began to glow.

My love is in the counting house,
my love is on the make.
They say my love lies bleeding,
I say the wound's a fake.
Some say blood will gather,
but that's an old mistake.

Our lad is in the haystack
and his lady's with him too.
Pigs are in the parlour,
drunk as morning dew.
It's passing late for April Fool,
the devil missed his cue.

As I walked out one morning,
in the merry month of June,
I found my Lady on her cross
beneath a bleeding moon.
In God's name, where's the sense in that?
It doesn't fit the tune.

One misty, moisty morning,
I was walking in the rain,
met an old girl, on the road,
who laid me in the drain.
Now the stars are falling,
she'll not be back again.

Plodge

Gan plodgin. Gan for a plodge. Magic plosives
conjure paddle, plunge and plop so,
how come England missed it? Plodgin in puddles n clarts?
Smart arse reckons it came from plod
but that's not liquid, not viscous. There's got to be goo.

Even down at the coast, there's slurry, grainy,
sand syrup that jiggers your toes.
Mud, ripe as a fart, at the old, crooked gate. Cattle
have plodged up the cack. Or simple
mud, at the wet edge of town, is perfect for plodgin.

Word made for snuggling. *Gan plodgin.* Mouth to mouth
word like a deep kiss. *Howway pet.*
Let's gan for a bit plodge. Take me hand pet. I'll unloose
your shoes, peel your socks off. A word
for undressing, when no-body's watching, wrap round you,

cuddle up close to, word to make you unfaithful,
seducing your tongue. Before you
know it, your whole body, naked as moonshine has plodged
through a swamp live with words, each one
  tight as a lover's hug.

Home Is Where The Word Is

Sounding down throat, heart, lung, bowel, groin,
her long, dark vowel of the soul rhymes
        with gnome and tome,
to bubble and grub with worms in Eden's loam.

Word with ancestry and baggage. Tongue-
        thick, warrior word,
spoken through Beowulf's helmet lineage bronze,
rhyme-rich, chiming in hearth-light with harm.

A north word, for untold thousands of tears.
        Our best guess –
haimi – oiling her mouth with smiles,
or lovers, riding home on August straw.

Kids on yard in colliers' black fleck,
booting a tin-can football over dialect's
        low brick wall.
These two, looping in lust, under hawthorn

shelters of sighs, on a heap they'll never reclaim.
Revellers, half-dressed, half-pissed, in light
        half-remembered,
gannin hyem to a leaf-ghost Viking bed.

This is her word, striving in stranger's earth,
        a borderland
thriving on outlaw fells, where fugitives bark.
Her warm lips mouth, on mine, their mother's hum.

Hull Brewery Chimney

Finger a phallus and reeking of hops,
as a child it would make me feel sick.
Mum said it were bad for us
and dad kept quiet.

Smell hovered over the city at times,
like gas, or plague, or sin.
Something to be avoided
when weather rumbles in.

Rose from an inner sanctum,
beyond our bridge of sighs.
Remains now, a singular monument,
while memory runs dry.

Words began fermenting
songs in a barrel of light.
Mum watched frowning, beyond the pale,
while dad kept quiet.

Party Game

Here's my promise, pass it round,
as long as you hear the music sound,
as long as pipe and fiddle play
over the hills and far away.

When you feel the music stop,
peel off the paper, let it drop.
When fiddle and pipe no longer play,
throw these ancient skins away.

Wrapped in parchment, bleached white,
inside is a creature of shivering light.
Wrapped in leaves of autumn words,
something that carols and dances with birds.

Wrapped in a veil, or baby's caul,
inside is a beating word that hauls
on sheets and spars and sails; clowns;
rides the ocean, never drowns.

Wrapped in leather, soft as hurt,
inside is a heart.
Wrapped in gossamer fine as mist,
inside is a boy who's never been kissed.

Wrapped in bandages around,
inside is a wound.
Wrapped in silk that shimmers in stars,
whatever's inside, is yours.

And one last parcel, naked as fright,
inside is the night.

The Dancer

Dance to the magic, dance to the moon,
dance to the fiddler, dance in tune.
Who'll be my partner? Who will dance with me,
over the mountains, over the sea?

'Not I,' said the wind, 'my step is like lead.'
'Not I' said the rain, 'there are knives in my tread.'
Oh the pipe and fiddle they whirl and play
over the hills and far away.

'Not I' said the lightning, 'my bolt is ablaze.'
'Not I' said Jack Frost, 'I am set in my ways.'
Yet pipe and fiddle, they whirl and play
over the hills and far away.

So who'll be my partner, who will dance with me
under the shade of the greenwood tree?
Pale, grey ghosts on a parlour wall
leap and dance at midnight's call.

Shadow in a sunset, glimmer in the snow,
figures in firelight flash and glow.
My hand gripped tight, the night enchants
me, whisks me away in winter's glance.

So I'll dance with the magic, dance with the moon,
dance to the dark night's eldritch tune.
Be my partner. Dance with me
over the silvery soul of the sea.

Remembrance

The beeches are felled.
Nine years I passed them, every day,
grey veterans, crowding the road for a pension,
cluttering space where the hill fell away
to an unseen river.

Determined to spot
passing princes, a duchess or two,
gone now, tumbled with alien evergreens;
one last roll in gleaners' hay and they've
cashed in their chips.

The road runs naked
now to a terrible sky. Old-time campaigners
trundle their carts under fading legends;
one medal yet remains, hooked
to a rainbow ribbon.

Cut Grass

When we were kids, council workman
rode on a grass cutter chasing the dragons,
just like Sir Lancelot. We hunted unicorns
        just round the corner.

Cut grass releases an odour of innocence,
earth's mother perfume, playtime fragrance.
Trimmed edge, a mown verge exposes anguish
        close to oblivion.

Days we would roll in it, swallow it, throw it,
scrub someone's face in it, stuff it down girls' backs.
Stung by a tingle of skin, soon we'd die for it
        quicker than tasting.

Oh, we could revel like dogs in it, wallow and
breathe in it. Savouring summer we'd sup on it,
lick up the stuff. We were made for it.
        Wounded angels,

Ian and Maureen, Paul and Anita,
Josephine, Margaret, Christopher rising
green as they bleed, young as clover, marked by it,
        too deep for cleaning.

Scent of a season gets into your gut,
raising grace and fable phantoms;
lust for the rot in it never forgotten –
        cut, green skin.

Build A Bonfire

Autumn bonfire, rake up debris,
weed and branches, leaf and grass,
screws of paper, heart of darkness –
dowsed in turps, it's bound to catch.

Pyracantha, holly, berberis,
knives and prickles, thistle, thorn –
all that wounds and tears and ruptures,
heap and burn, lad, heap and burn.

Flame unfettered like a dancer,
fire silks and sequin sparks
pirouettes around the garden,
gold vermilion in her heart.

Watching from an upstairs window,
catching capers in the smoke,
Rumplestiltskin in the bat light
hopes to keep us in the dark.

Now in shadow, on the bonfire,
I can see your hair ablaze
and your song roars like a candle,
through this micklemass of days.

The Allotment

Travel by tandem, neat as a whistle, Saturday
made for two, for three, spade and hoe
strapped to the frame, matinee, musket, lance,
Lee Enfield; me in my sidecar, zapping the council
    houses, bright as Bayko.

Whizz by the school for boys with too much mischief,
girls already tough in their infinite stardust.
Glance by bike shop and barber, swing by the road
to the docks where tank engines rumble their dragon-beat steam
    through my dreams.

Somewhere, I can never find again,
a thin back-lane runs to ground set aside
for those in need of earth and country. Tandem
rode us into space. Was there a shed?
    Gone now. Out of my head, and the place, and the land.

Warm, earth odour remains, spuds and carrots
fresh as dirt, onions and cabbages rooting
brain and gut to the land. A rough, nail-jarring,
claypot rasp, cracks easy and shatters
    on bonfires of memory.

Hack and chop, grave, spade slice through Holderness
clay. Clod-breaking scrape of Dutch hoe snags flint.
Chalk nuggets jag at weed roots. And I know
they were there, war-wise, turtle calm,
    in their brief allotment.

I recall the Eden tree deformed,
an old world crumbling in her roots, low limb
I could climb on, sit and read *The Eagle*,
sniff bonfire bomb sites round the city,
    smell flesh roots, green leaves for the pot.

Hot tang of the way things always would be.
Fat oak body rubs under my naked thighs,
rough as all outdoors. Bark-pelt and Babel
trunk, fissured in lost canals, tower
    up to a crown of infinite leaf.

Each vein trace a poem, flown free
of shifting earth, clean away to the great,
    un-landed surface of our moon.

The Approximate Boy

Once upon a time, when the world was straight,
soup for dinner on Mondays
(because it was easy and washday)
trolleybuses hummed like change on wires up to granny's.
Slaps of estuary gulls rang flat
on stone sky, squealed their communion,
winter's bread and dripping,
warm, dark-morning, syrup-of-tea-swigging breakfast.

Once, in a land where the gas poker roared,
garden trench-line roses
(brought, like history and jokes,
with barbs in a brass tin's medal hoard, from grandpa's)
snored, like an old man's ghost by the fire.
Mum steamed sacrament fish,
for white sauce, in Friday's kitchen.
Grandpa sang hymns, in his photo, on the piano.

Out on a limb in the wilderness now,
in a fog that stank of Iceland's
cod road end, out west,
an approximate boy pitched tent, in sight of home,
feeling the tingle of being alone,
boy on a verge, in wind,
shivering, under mind,
sprawled on his oilcloth, reeking of tar and pitch.

Once, on a time I can see quite straight,
an approximate boy, under canvas,
lived beyond his compass,
in sight of home, on a verge, where three roads faltered.
And over the pavement, blind in light,
lost in his best friend's *Beano*
(and grandpa's last inferno) our
nearly-man trembles, while the bent world alters.

Boys From The Flat Land

Were there three of us that day, or four
(I can't remember)
trudging paths we knew, through Holderness clay
and wintry hedge
stripped of berry and leaf, by bird and wind?

January dark, and ploughland clods
degrade the edge,
blade-sheen peaks to silt ripples, under grey,
north-rain-driven
nails, crazed rooks in ministerial flocks.

Primitive Methodist ranter clones of vengeance,
rise from miniature
dales under clay, swirl round our heads, like nagging
sins. Sleet-flecked
gulls, in steel-oilcloth grey, strafed our Gomorrah,

streamed an icy, Baltic passage in rain sheets.
Lapwing flaunted
draggle crowns, peewitting over grim,
East Riding towns,
Tharlesthorpe, Owthorne, Ravenser Odd. Winter

came screaming over the dying and dead. Boulder
clumps of barely
innocent days, plunge headlong from crumbling cliffs,
crash, in imperial ruin.
We are the boys from the flat land, drained by old

monk-dykes, to a thin chalk-river. Gabble and burble
language few understand.
We are the boys from the flat land, mumbling
claysong. Words
tumble down to the broad, flat, Humber sewer.

Travelling Home From Granny's

A Litany for 1950s Hull

Dark city, river-land, fog rolls.

Alien plays
from wireless worlds
moth-post the lamp
light galaxies.

Church shells reek
still in their fire ways.

City roll, dark bomb, fog sites.

Come river brand full strength,
cold as a coal house,
twice black and fish stinking
wet brick and iron cold
steam smoke last
allotment bonfires.

Blue bus, river-way, fog bombs.

I just climbed aboard;
the driver pulled down
the brown blind in his cab
and fare table city names
read as exotic
as islands behind glass
chrome-locked by catches.

Cycle packs
hunt at the crossings.

Fog-city dark, roll lantern wise.

And soon we shall pass
the second hand
re-cycling shop;
for now but, the tide is in,
north bridge is up,
my road lifts her dark arm
starward.

Parish Records

Outside the Co-op, snow lies childhood deep
in fluffy dumps. The telephone box, dumb
and deaf as hope,
glows red against the shambling traffic hum,
dreaming business. No-one hears a peep.

The pillar box is stuffed to overflow
with winter news. Messages of light
see fit to glow,
while Emma's mobile, silent as the night,
betrays a lack of signal through the snow.

Under the looming chestnuts' monstrous frame
lie broken shells. Their rotten spines betray
memorial stone.
Old poppies rage like ghosts in angry snow.
Dale picks one last conker for the game.

Our parish notice-board reveals the place
and time to be. A stranger stops to look
and break her race.
Searching for stars, she spies the shadow rooks
who flap their gloom across an upturned face.

Hoping for angels in the parish books,
she treads pale feathers in a mess of grace.

Bronze Horizons

Northern twilight rounds a darksome day.
Trees are black as dim, remembered dreams.
Floods of flame keep night at bay
and hills are shadow, cast on wintry streams.
Vixen prints her legend on the moor.
Salmon slide along the river's mark.
Heron prince, he pins the farther shore
while squirrels hoard their songs against the dark.
From bronze horizons, winter's guest rolls down
to find the pub, the butcher, and the store,
to make a halfway heart and home in town
where there's a gap, a chink, an open door.
And far beyond these grey, unguarded fells,
there jangle faintly, fond remembered bells.

Saison En Soleil

Folk mark summer's end with fire;
come in their cars, camper vans, four by fours,
wobble on motor-bikes for a double
drench of goodwill and pineau, driving
into the dark.

Weave their sun-drunk farandole,
meandering green-brown oyster channels
rich with mud-bright lust. Nod
their wink at virgin egrets
on fine bone stilts.

Hot summer people mingle and sweat
in the little port, balancing lives down narrow
quays, where boats hold hands and knock
their hearts on warm stone.
Two by two,

squash through small, familiar squares.
Street lights hang pregnant, yellow blooms
from drooping lamp-posts. Gathering artists
fill scented salons with hymns to a drunken
saison en soleil.

Comfortable lovers share
a sweetness of *crêpes*. In sludge-light oils,
they are tasting one another's year
in craze-glaze moonshine. These days, we are all
waiting for fireworks.

The Naming Of Plants

i.m. Ken Fenton, Teacher of Biology, Hull Grammar School.
For Paul, Steve and all the others, 1962-1969

We loved you more than physics or chemistry,
called you the Mekon, bane of the galaxy,
feared, in spite of being small
and green, by earthlings after the fall
though not, it goes without saying, Dan Dare,
nor us in the sixth form, to be fair.
High, sloping forehead, distinctive as formalin
named you in love and a rush of adrenalin.
Thus we approached the biology lab
when verse was vile and music fab.
General science was never your forté
but such was our lot, at your hands, for a First year.

Sodium, malleable, ductile, a metal
so reactive it trembles in oil.
One fragment in water shatters the molecule,
breaks all bonds of earthly rule.
Energy, that year, was a tad
too much. Blast Dan Dare. (And his dad.)
Blasted one pneumatic trough
to smithereens – I heard the staff
still guffawed long ages after. So
grow gospels on human nature. We
remember, we who fell
behind the bench but lived to tell
and better tell the myth you made,
celebrate your escapade
some fifty years on down the line.
Unlikely heroes gild our time.
Disciples muttered, surfaced, scattered,
peppered with pot and shots of laughter.

Your role in the creation mystery
needs recognition. Wispery
miracle after fertilisation.
Cometh the lesson: invagination!
A hollow ball of cells turns in
on itself – mandala spins.
Somehow, I've never forgotten the Word,
or how you demonstrated. God!

Your body stretched, arms out, reached up
over and inward. A rubbery pup,
or swimmer beached on Eden's earth.
Your shirt rode up, a gaping mirth
of girth, out of a waistband swivel,
exposing God's brown, hairy navel.

Your saints and angels all were plants.
Your breath was botany. Chance
existence brought us to your door.
Seldom saw you in a gown
or in assembly. You and God,
I guess, were frequently at odds
and you, when tired, sad or pissed
probably thought Him a physicist.

Lastly, when we were elder statesmen,
in the prep room, revising late, then
you initiated kiddies
in the fear of God and bodies.
A three foot ruler cracked their doom
on a sacred desk, at the front of the room.
Nonchalant then, you wandered back
to front our fears with chuckle and crack.
Your fond grin sparkled ear to ear:
Put the shits up them for the next six years.

So now you've shuffled off, unpickled,
shocked, surprised or disappointed,
are you in or out of reckoning?
How's your new embryo appointed?
Your entry into any form
of paradise would generate
such turbulence at break of term
too violent to speculate.

I know you despaired of my song and dance. Still –
I'm known for some skill in the naming of plants.

Made By The Ladies Of The Church

They called her Salome,
that severed head on a pedestal.
Full savoy cabbage,
provocative, loose leaves

barely cover her shoulders,
hips and damsons necklace,
pearls, the nation's poet
ought to be warming

for each little godling
bursting from tight-laced bosoms.
Eye-berries, pinned to their sockets, weep
real tears of Burgundy blood.

An overflow of passion on the altar.
Chillies and curly kale in her bonnet
disguise our mother's, old-crone,
creature familiar,

wearing nowt but a white shift habit,
under the surgeon's knife.
They called her Salome,
my lover's head on a platinum salver,

weeping and bleeding,
in pride of place by the door.
Don't ignore her.
Harvest is barely begun.

Limelight

Once, it would have been real lime,
burning stone, pearl of light
ablaze above the ranks. Caustic flame,
in brilliance, banks
the neutron blessing of your song.

And I must track you and your cat
to the singer's rock. Spangled night
Guides a lover progress through black rows.
My hawser yokes, photon
ropework, to a blind light-maker.

Lantern moths, in a dark wood, flit
where three ways meet, paths untrod:
one to a stage, one to midnight's
audience, one light
performance pins you to your red rock.

I have the best view of all, throw you
lumen's cloak, your moment's glow.
My perfect pain knows you, wave
and cadence, shape and grace.
Light is mine, shines on you,

lacing your hair, soaking through pores
to a pool of eyes, refracting
in time's waste, your bright, rhyme radiance.
One click provides a brittle shell,
faience fabergé, a spell,

a rhymer's tongue, glamour's bell.
Light is mischief's insect pin
to hold you, till I switch the line. Sleep now,
cat and comedy's dark logic,
until some flaming author works his magic.

Dr Who

Dr Who stepped out of monochrome fog
one day after the world shot a hole in its head
which proved to be massively bigger
inside and full of horror, while,
here on the outside, it was only a head
cradled and bleeding in her lap.

He stepped across our fantasy. Life's
anachronism lay claim to names
and faces we long to hold
in our hands. Open the door to a box of
impossibility – a machine whose bosom
rising, flickers, falls and hums

the love song of ages – paradox. Imaginary,
angel numbers perch on a pin-head, infinite
square roots of minus a heart
in the attic. He has been nailed, ten thousand
times, to English greenwood's golden bough.
A messenger from paradise,

betrayed by fallen lords, furthers the endless
labours of a flawed, forgotten god.
Perfection and humanity
rock on a pendulum.
No longer dare to hope to solve equation,
screen, a disc, googols of answers.

Rainbow singularity, now
she dances ever more nimbly, scarf, recorder,
clapped-out car, guitar or
hint of a kiss. Promise to keep faith
with two hearts, changing face each time
the universe shifts gear. She'll promise
  to live forever, so we don't have to.

A Lesson In Sodium

Memory fragile,
malleable,
ductile.

The master dropped his nugget in our bucket.

Exploding water,
sodium ruptures rain pearls,
splits our meniscus.

It's elemental,
bending a greenstick vision.

A glittering gobbet to burst our potential.

Kept in a jar on the shelf,
our boy-bright pebble
drowned in glutinous liquor
under safe oil.

Picked on a whim by clinical tongs,
kids in a bundle wait on corruption
by his wisdom.

Expecting to be rinsed in concentric ripples,
we leap for cover,
caught in the tumult of aftershock,
his alchemy of laughter.

Edinburgh

This musical of time gone by,
when comedy, like coal, was king,
women tied to the tracks, babies
flattened in steam trouser presses and villains
wore vampire capes, twirled grease-black moustaches.

Dark uniforms, scarlet, white
insignia bound us to a stop.
Woman, tight black leather skirt,
handbag unclasped, violated.
Orchestra, flying over the stage, had something

of old Shostakovich about it. Outside,
the Christmas market bustled and burped,
dazzling night, exploding light.
Ferris Wheel spun you heaven-high,
back to a gutter of bratwurst, a sweetness of Glühwein.

Whipped, like a fact, the Star Flyer
whizzed screaming ghosts on wing and prayer
to fling their long-forgotten wisdom
round and round the cartoon totem,
antique city, at ease with its helter-skelter.

Fairytale grotto, nothing remotely
Palestinian about it. Strange old man,
children skating with penguins,
carved, wooden, family groups in an animal
outhouse, refugees in a cardboard shack.

Dancers tapped away to the signs.
Our hero muffed his lover's lines.
Heroine dazzled and died of drugs. Finale.
Drop loose change in disaster's bucket.
Beggar backs against the wall are invisible

under grey-shadow hoods of suspicion.
Not sure where leather woman
got to. Or why it matters to me.
She was never part of our story.
Would never belong to our music, or dance.

Lurids patrol their roller coaster,
carousel gallopers, grinning, spinning
high over city and sheep on fells.
Turn your frosted faces
to the unbelieving, stationary stars.

Pater Noster

Myra Elizabeth Medd (1914-1942)

Our father lost his first wife in the war,
not to the floods of flame or satan bombs,
crooked planes or rape of angel hoards –
that first leave, bonfire of anthems barely begun,
cold consumption swallowed her in his bed.
Woke to find her dead. And her name never spoken
after, gleaned from his army paybook (widowed)
in parenthesis, his broken token.

Had they, I wonder, one last lap of love
round her never-to-wrinkle, rise or ripen belly?
Last round of sighs that drowned him in her floods
in a world made flesh? And is this muse unsavoury?
Or was he lost in her great ark of pain
unrainbowed, grounded on her virgin peaks,
agony and emptiness, bad rain
leaking from her lips in spots and kisses?

From his armchair by the fire, we shared
her image, once, enough to let the dart
penetrate, where she had nailed him,
showers of sparks that light and dance and hurt not.
I saw this world that was not me, and she
was blood and bone, hot breath in my heaving lung.
Shameless, she played cat's cradle with my dreams,
weaving, twisting threads in a tangled song.

One word, one cenotaph, tabula rasa,
her melody a symphony of no's,
no name, no photograph, no ring, no story,
chasing vision down grey, smoke-stack rows.
And then, one brief encounter on the page,
a wintry tale, whispered by hedge and furrow,
never sung, though shadow leap and rage –
no smile, no kiss, desire, no tomorrow.

She's become this traveller's hill-top stone,
engraved with rings and cups, heaven's grimy womb
where sad men fear to knock. I cut her out,
saddle her with pale whelps got in ice,
flows of frost, innocence and grief.
An image once worth worship, now so rarely
noticed, dances madly round the stars,
hauling my tongue's tide, one dark, fiery wife.

And Grandpa Smoked His Pipe

I know now he was dying, in our house,
    in a chair by the fire.
And that was the biggest thing ever to happen
    in our house, right up

to your miscarriage. He levered his grey, long legs
    in front of our real,
coal fire, scared to a gas poker blaze. Fat toad
    memory croaks,

his woollen waistcoat warmed my fingers, though ash
    fell like rose petals,
after the last, great frost. And the radio
    spoke of another

strike. And I wondered at that, because I knew
    about matches (which
are dangerous). Meanwhile, the woman in another
    room steamed fish,

hissing like the devil in a pressure cooker. Must have been
    Good Friday. There would be
mashed potato, and thick, white, glutinous,
    parsley sauce.

I should have been too young to remember, but know now
    a face, not a photograph,
stares at me out of a post-war, newsreel jingle.
    And sun shone like billyo,

over the clay-coloured roofs that sprang up
    poppy fields of apologies.

Spring Morning

Tom Medd – 1915-1980

That morning forged a landscape scarified:
steel sky beaten blue to a stunned grin,
fields bruised green, a wheel of lapwing turned
on the heel of spring. Trees,
like my father, blizzard black, recall his passing,
one last snap of winter.

Rollicking mischief in sticky buds,
this racketing angel, puck of the gold stream,
picks roots and noses. Non-starter god,
holy-smoking rascal
with a nose for fires, lights his giggle,
upturns the globe like a tortoise.

Happen he saw the clay-cold, winter leaves
gather in swamp ditches, blown where mould,
maggot and beetle, hold their festival
under the spider's wall.
Happen he sniffed incense in the urchin church
that claps red summer's bell.

Stood in his triangle plot of land
where we buried the cat, built bonfires, grew
green hearts, like cabbages, after the war;
tilled his creed's dividend,
watching friends from his garden gate
and the year turn round, already late.

I know he heard our coltsfoot sun burst
like a squib, and lark psalm praises ring
blue Sunday sky. He made trees
belly forth his twinkle,
saw his devil on shrew's feet
tiptoe through roses like a kid.

I know he saw the urchin in his mould
stick up two fingers at a grubby world,
revelation's shed-load of muck.
The March clown flew his kite,
lit god's beard, drew on his pipe and,
stooping, set the tortoise on his feet.

The Pitman Painters And Van Gogh

Woodhorn allotments have whippets,
green pigeon crees and a pit.
Montmartre has Paris, absinthe
windmills, a terrace for sightseeing.

And someone (caught in a Camelot picture)
works in a garden of weed and relish,
pulling courgettes for the salad,
(nine bean rows, and a daub of promise).

Caught in a border ballad,
echoes of charges and rockets,
I'll sing with winding gear, engine fog,
five, racketing coal board wagons,

brown beer (no boulevard café), four dogs,
mum with a pram and a toddler,
house-end walls, plastered with passé
adverts for wisdom and jam.

And a man on a bike is rounding
a kerb on his demob bum.
Dad, or the me I was meant to be,
pedalling faster than love

on a bend, his last attempt
in poet oils (crow's rag under his thumb)
to swing round a painter's curve,
on paradise, allotment wheels.

Hull Fair, October 15th 1966

The Big Wheel counts her minutes down,
though I am terrified of heights.
But as we soar above the town,
the Big Wheel counts our minutes down.
The Caterpillar smothers all
in darkness, and the night is gone.
Your butterfly outstrips the lights,
but I am terrified of heights.

Ethel Fletcher

Nov 27 1885 – Sept 01 1972

Granny. That's no name for a woman. That's an old sewing machine
treddling comfort blanket threads of catastrophe.
Smart range, polished black as November,
forging tomorrow sparks through conflagration.
Three in one,
goddess in mufti.
Girl dancing light through a century's gate.
Child in still waters,
paddling dream in the shallows, dabbling toes
under duck noses,
out on a fish-bright, city's edge chimney-shadow.
That's jester tomfoolery, trawled round the fairground, for a woman
who's gold-brown hair turned June day sun
to fire and fun,
when the daft, old year was lost, on a carousel nobody knew
had stopped turning.

That's no name for limb-joy, lover's embrace, lost music, lost
glamour,
lost dance, her long song silent. She was two-up-two-down, plus
the kitchen
she called a shed, in spite of the gas.
A tap between her and Uncle Ernie. Toilet
outside in yard,
next to the coal house.
Syllables for a weekend back to front,
where I slept in dad's
old allotment, seed bed. Sleeping with shadows.
Dodging the enemy,
behind marble washstand, basin and ewer.
Baptismal liquor in a railway font. And a bedroom lightswitch
dangle near my skull, black button
to click off all
those greyscale paybook, lost-in-parenthesis, dead,
unwanted years.

Granny. That's a one room, living room, chaise-long, black-leather
boat-slide,
mountain-slope ride. That's a rocking chair, nodding chair,
doze-by-the-blaze chair. Dad snack, Windsor
back, great cost engine-chuffing, black-stuff-huffing proof
of desire.
Mantelpiece moniker.
Pot dog, candlestick, nimble Jack, look out!
Nick's in the cupboard
with a tea caddy. Tick tock click, dear old clock,
over the heart-fire
riding the range, mocking the stranger, out on far
horizons I've never set eyes on. A streamline Pacific on
a mineral line, shunting stock
to a siding.
Brass ash tray glows with dottle she'd not blow away till
the gun tune stopped.

One clean special room barely entered, deep-smelling yesterpetal
fragrance I can never place, where she kept her gold brown
dazzle, her invisible dance, kept
her boiler-breasted, engine-thundering, steam beat,
coupling rod,
her great red, lost-great-heart,
calamity of a man, forty years on,
wrong side of the clock.

Testament

We stumbled on a market in a small, town square
where two huge, continental rivers meet.
Boulangerie, patisserie, fromage
and fish. Raw meat curing. Flies
and blood. Wains of fruit and veg.

Vast, mundane commodities being
human snuggled under *bel ombrage.*
Parchment verses, dry as old patriarchs.
Great, green plane trees, dark as a pulpit,
crowded like fallen angels round the church.

One stall of dresses caught your eye,
cold, black, legless models, crow saints
fixed their charcoal gaze on humanity.
One dress, I knew in an instant, was you,
shape and figure, smooth, dark imago

clothed in your chrysalis. All day you wore it.
Blues and rainbow tessellating brilliance,
shot with light. Tesseracts of your multitudes
jostled for songspace in Burgundy sun.
All day, you dazzled through crowd gloom.

We led your song down ancient lanes.
Rarely-open doors trilled on rime-rust hinges.
Arches rumbled in their cut of sky.
Dined early. *Boeuf bourguignon.* Flavour distilled
on a low heat, all day. Tenderness fell away

in our mouths. That night, fifty years fell away.
Your rare skin, laced with blue fire, burned
my fingers. Dazzled by your moment's flare,
I saw two rivers meet, in a land's great heart,
and wear away the old fool's ruined arch.

Verdun sur le Doubs

Your Wedding Gift

for Diane

Your wedding gift was an earthenware casserole dish
glazed to a dazzle; brown as a chestnut outside,
shades of all those coffees we shared inside;
lives in a cupboard. I'd always assumed it was empty.

Now I know you filled it from warm, damp earth;
picked off beetles that tickle, the odd leather jacket,
lice; washed clean slug-veins in waves we played in;
scrubbed it with sand I had written your name in, that summer.

You pared away rind we grew for protection. Now,
I recognise intricate cuts you made
with bright instruments, before dicing the lot into pieces;
these you arranged in your pot before adding seasoning.

Innocence sharper than ginger. Cinnamon, warm
as a stranger's hand held under sycamores. Cloves,
to numb the jangled nerves of childhood's ache.
You fired all with peppercorns of kindness.

Avoiding the curdled excess of deceit, you brewed this
in moderate heat for three years. We dined last night.
The meal was a pleasure long-prepared, something
slow-cooked, barely warm at all, all day.

This morning I cleaned your pot, put it away.
So long, since last we met, it sat in that cupboard.
Finally, I understand. It was always
full, always nourishing, all these years.

Miscarriage

Agony loads the air with chrysanthemums.
Odours, like a dark star, leach their pollen
into my bloodstream. Coal-black snowflakes etch
design that doubled you, needle under brain rind
picking synapses till they jangled.

Pain was your remit, hailing a star's existence.
Years, we believed it impossible. Now, the forensic,
evident, tell-tale, ghost-stain mocked our sheets.
Can that be how it works? Each of us loitering
out in chaos, waiting on blueprints of glory?

Well. We were all fingers and thumbs and yet,
your wanderer came calling, took up residence.
Had we guessed, we'd have sheltered the spark from catastrophe,
sat by the fire, hand-join cups around
your tiny glittering. Oh, we'd have breathed on you

all the delight we could muster! So there you are,
intake of sudden breath, one butterfly word,
or a moth, whose wing beats bring down tyrants. And when
we turn on shadow, unseen hand on a shoulder,
silent rumour of night stock, in empty gardens,

this remains, your twenty-four year echo.
Once, we must have loved enough,
    attracting a star.

Autumn Incident

A697 – the Coldstream road

Drizzle greased the six-nine-seven. A Citroën
rounded heaven's bend; no scourge or slap of speed,
only a swerve that spun his wheels
on shallow turf. A rotten verge
rejected him, spurned his advances, propelling him into
the dirt-dark, brute-blue Transit.

Steel fume and sound-chaff choreographed
a sodden thump, orchestrating road noise, radio,
wiper swish and heater hum,
then a dull-dunsh, stomach crunch that jarred
my gut. Whip-top world turned slowmo
pirouette, into the ditch.

The dark van stopped on an instant. I remember
endless moments pondering turn or swerve, then gentle
braking. Stop for good, three whispers
short of silence. Came the emergency
legions, green as spring in daffodil wagons,
brought me chills in the drizzle.

Appointments missed. A pointless pas de deux
was all that mattered, great grey grunt of collision, land's
refusal. Oh, and one man's benediction
                – He's dead.
                                        I remember
rain soaking grass, seeping through
inadequate jackets, chilling bone and standing
alone with autumn scarlet,

yellow, blue confusion. Death came whispering
over the static airwaves, tapped on my grease-marked windscreen,
(bought me a tell-tale pint in the pub),
penned his official report in life's grey court.
October's broken waters lumped in a ditch,
with an after-birth of bracken.

Ceremony For John

Cold morning,
Newbiggin church
on the point,
and a bitter North Sea.

Below the pulpit,
one brick on a table,
his builder's trowel,
this broken scaffolding pole.

His football boot,
wedding smile photograph
and candle fire, lit
by one of his two sons

Fishing boat tapestries
rock on their kneelers.
A miner's lamp
remembers shadows.

Stone heads watch
through chancel walls.
And the nave is black with hurting,
speckle-white faces foam

on a raggy sea. Hymns are hard
to carry, until the voice of a seagull
cheers a Saturday boy's goal,
out on the park. Over our shoulders,

October sun scrambles up, scuffs his knees
on the stone sill, to peer at us all
through stained glass windows,
with fond, anxious face.

Saturday 26th October 2013

Congregation Of Rooks

Why do so many dark rooks flock
to congregate on a stone-dead tree?
Mornings I find them, hooked on this broken
bone hand, grasping air and sea.
Raucous familiars, bubble froth tatters,
black earth breath, noting my passing.
Unholy governors, hungry debaters
gather in shawls round naked shoulders.

Shreds of gloss wing, sleek tail wedge
weld night's veil to a skeleton elm.
Some deep inflammation kindles
ghost buds murmuring under the skin.
Hags astride their monstrous weapon,
punctual as spring, summon
whisper and prayer, hurly-burly
laughter for their pilgrim parley.

Could these rag and bone marauders
out on a limb, peck summer's eyes,
flense love's rib clean as concrete,
loud as the urgent buzz of flies?
Why should these shoddy moppers up
of time flock to their lobby whips?
Fled from a land that'll never be mine
ladies, I never elected their kind.

It seems I've stumbled blind upon
guerrilla cells, while holes in my skin
pricked by purveyors of rhyme and song
are letting the girls from dead worlds in.
Their songs are behind me (never look back)
stealing a heart's march over the wreck.
Sniggers of dirt and dancing memory
lay out dark lines of my ancestry.

The Park School

Started work in Ashington in January.
Just the worst time of year for a change: dark
settling over the soul, snow threatening
blanket-cold-smothering, and the children
hunting in packs, for promise of work, in the park.

Hope-grown architecture in a colliery school;
cloister corridors, open quad
long since closed, echo the union years
with composition, sums and laws,
measuring existence by the rule.

Once-upon-a-time, coal-stained brick
designed in cuboid symmetry blocks,
scaled pantiled, orange heaven, line and prism.
Sixty years of new September
faces wait for their first red tick.

Two Vals

Two Vals. Little Val, Big Val. Valeries.
Cleaners too full of mischief, laughter,
and language, Morecambe and Wise. Been there,
school immemorial, dragging a world

un-wonted through my classroom, tickled and dusted.
If I were soon enough, they'd be there,
having made the knackered brickwork
good as could be for our painful efforts.

Moppers-up of ill- considered moments.
And once I set my frail birds free,
they'd be back, vixen and hen,
scooting through corridors, hunting paper planes,

chewed pencils, broken words and rulers,
early drafts of childhood – hovering
misplaced, good intentions. Valeries.
Two shakes of mischief's tail. And this,

they'd tell me, is all bollocks. One Valerie
was chewed ends, picking at rope strands,
virus threads in milk or thin,
hair floaters in golden beer. A fine,

bone china egg, lacquered with fireworks,
finery, frivolous folderols shimmering,
ringing true as pigeon coo,
through old brick. Sharp as a note to crack jokes,

inside Valerie twisted hemp
anguish, hot as a Chinese burn.
The day we drove to meet the train
at Hexham, for our daughter's homecoming,

little Val hanged herself. Shards blaze
unfettered. Misplaced, treasured frescoes,
damaged, early drafts of mischief,
tell me, this is all bollocks.

Guzintas

Please miss, Ah divvent de guzintas
Ah divvent de guzintas cos Ah'm thik
no it's rite miss
        me Ah'm thik me
        thik as shit.   No it's trew.

Ah cannat read   Ah cannat rite
        Ah de worksheets an cularinin
                Ah de spelincards   Ah can spel
                        dog an cat an crap   Ah can spel

wordsawon wotsit miss
        wotsitwon sillywot
                srite miss sillybul
                        Ah can de them mostly but

Ah cannat de never
        an mebbes an tumorrer
                an tumorrer miss an mirrer

Ah divvent de mirrer
        on akownt o the ows

Ah divvent de big words miss
        Ah gerrem in me ed burra
                cannagerramowt

Ah divvent de mafmatix
        Ah de addizups
Ah divvent de sighance cos
        ther woz this fire an
Ah divvent de jografi cos
        Ah bust the gloab an
Ah divvent de histricos
        me dad sez wots the yuso kings
an Ah divvent de frenshojorman cos
        thay shud orl speek inglish miss
Ah yooster de compewtas
        but now Ah've got me eksboks
Ah divvent de musik cos
        them little blak tadpoles miss
                the buggers never keep still an

Ah divvent de art cos
        paintsexpensiv

Ah de de litter if miss dikson aksus
        she's nice
                an wen damiun werksisel in er lessens
                        Ah givim a dedleg
                              that fettlesim

Ah de pakinup anerands
        an chairs an ditenshun on mundis
                burra Ah divvent de guzintas

Wot miss??

Yer meentersay ye divvent knaa???

Onest miss   teechas   Ah thort
        teechas new evrythin miss

Mister mildenorl sez
Derek de guzintas
        Ah ses wot
e ses guzintas derek
de guzintas
        Ah ses wot
e ses derek man

owmeny nines guzinta sickstyfree

Thats justa ferinstans cos
        Ah divvent de guzintas.

Derek's Wirds

wirdseye want
arowt in yard
ones down
boilerousteps
where Im
notaloutago
but the ball does

ones in
care takers garden

eddy kicked another right
ovvertheskool
interthekwod

summerthe rockwirds
get stuck like chud
underyerdesk
kanageritoff
like crap on yershoe

wirdseye want
arowt playinfooty
bildinaden inthewoods
wouldn't catch them
inside a glass room

they've got
too much sense

Literacy Level Three

Once upon a time
there was this metaphor,

Sharp as a new pin

That's a simile

Sorry

This metaphor sat by a puddle in the back lane,
squatted on a kerb, knees round his ears,
rolling a joint with one hand, stroking
his ear with the other ... that's his own ear

I know

Just checking   anyway
soon as he finished rolling
he tucked the joint behind his ear

Like a fag

Exactly   and he stared into the puddle

Right

And he stared into this puddle

You said that

Well he stared for a long time

Sorry   *And?*

Longer than that

Still staring?

I said didn't I   a long time.
Anyway   there he is thinking

Into this puddle?

Into this puddle when what does he see?

What?

Come up behind him like, reflecting

In the puddle?

In the puddle. What does he see but

The moon?

No

Not the harvest moon
like a ruddy farmer's face?

You've been reading again you'll go blind.

Well what? Not a hood with an AK47?
I know, a blond with lips red as cherries
and a top down to her

No

And

Certainly not

As big as

You'll definitely go blind

So she didn't kiss him
long and deep as China

I told you, similes can damage your health.

She didn't rip off her flimsy underwear,
like spider web, throw him back against
the canal bridge

Where did the ruddy canal come from?

Macclesfield. And have her wicked
but oh so long and moist and amorous
way with him?

Are you finished?

Very nearly.

Right then. Where was I?

Up against the brickwork under the canal bridge.

Will you shut up!

Sorry.

Well, moon monsters and honey trap
terrorists notwithstanding   he stared
in the puddle, saw this thing looming large as Friday
over his left shoulder, thought it was
Death on a Harley Davison
BUT
It was only a bleeding
frontal adverbial

School Bag

Three boys are running down our hill,
just after eight on a summer's morning,
one always in front, grows as he disappears.
All have rucksacks on their backs,
thumbs at each shoulder,
tucked under web-straps of childhood.
They run to school, sack stuffed tight,
homework, almost perfect.

Inside the bag, a ball for kicking
into a dream of playtime;
a scheme for camping, over the moor's edge,
under a huge rock left by the ice dragon;
mobile phone with a message from mum
about home time and strangers
    (maybe he'll read it in maths);
packed lunch, yoghurt, apple, sandwiches
    (maybe he'll eat it, out on the field,
    when the nice young teacher
    has her eye on the love play of sparrows).
Incomprehensibly, there's a note from a girl
he has to sit next to in French,
lost under trainers, a book about tractors,
last season's conker,
an incomplete set of footballer cards
and he doesn't know quite why he keeps it.
    (Her note.)

Running too fast now, jumping, feet pounding
rhythms I cannot quite register, unfluent, incoherent,
like French and maths and the signal from mum.
Even the one out front is not safe,
although he grows taller, the further he travels,
fades from our morning, growing
out of the inscape of his dream.

Summer today, but every day
they will be hurtling down our hill,
bouncing too fast round our corner. They may
skid on the gravel of other boys' lives
and fall on their bones.

Today's Lesson

There once was a boy
  who held out his hand
    so they gave him a number.
He lifted the gem to his lips and licked it.
No, they said. Idiot boy, you can't eat that.
But I am hungry, the boy replied
  and he bit it.
Good, they said. This
  is division.

There once was a girl
  who held out her hand
    so they gave her an alphabet.
She held it close to her heart and cuddled it.
No, they said. Silly girl, you can't love that,
  so she ripped out its eyes.
Good, they said.
  This is poetry.

There once was a teacher
  who held up her hand.
    This poem is all wrong, she said.
You gave the boy number but he needed letters.
The girl has an alphabet. She wanted calculus.
  So they shot her.
Good they said. This
  is the 21st Century.

Children held up their hands
    so they gave them certificates.
Mothers installed these tiger skins,
  like master-works,
  on living room walls.
No, they cried. Stupid women. These are to wear.
See, they have poetry, numbers and a gun.
  They know how to stand in line
    and who does not count.

Fixing Your Hard Drive

I am the boy who sits at the back of your class,
    shaking his head, talking too much.
I am the boy whose handwriting cannot be read,
    words misunderstood, diagrams
    all the wrong colour, shaded against the grain.

I am the boy who hears you, likes your voice
    miss, lipstick, new blue dress.
I am the boy, inside the boy, who nips
    the wimp for being a wimp, busts
    the nose of the boy who stole
    your purse miss, circles you
    on the class photo, on my bedroom wall.

I am the boy who doesn't belong
    to the books you write, songs you sing.
    Boy in your poem hates poems.
I am the boy who won't be here, long don't worry,
    you won't remember.
I am the boy who ought to be climbing walls,
    building a den in the woods,
    swimming in the mine pool.

I am the boy you can't ignore,
    running your messages, fixing
    your hard-drive, however you try.
I am the boy who understands dogs, ferrets,
    suicidal tendencies of rabbits,
    the closeness of rats.

I'm the boy, they tell you,
    who doesn't exist.

Balantsin 5s

Sit up straight he says
don’t swing on your chair
I swing back rocking
between desk and wall
between him and yes-
terday when it was
me and Tin on blades
we was fleein be-
tween honey bear and
here when triangles
have one hundred and
eighty reasons for
being anywhere
but somewhere between
his word and my wall
our time and this
minute when my heads
rocking between
his line and mine I
say there just intno
equilibrium

Amanda's 2nd Poem

God!

I hated school well you do when youre thick we
thats me and Sherilee Robinson we got sat
at the back if we could then she d read Seventeen
I d file me nails I had beautiful nails in them days
now theyre bitten to hell.

Young Mister Watson   golden hair   soft
blue eyes   I liked him   he was nice taught us
english   all that blood   Macbeth what a pillock
any fool could see his missus was
dead set on wearing the trousers   he should have   stood up
to her   when he had the chance   all that cloak
and dagger stuff with the spots   as for the weirdoes
Jesus   what were they on   you get them like that
down the lane of a Sunday night   I wrote
this poem once   miss Maunder told us how
everything started with a Big Bang only
in r k miss Craddock said it took seven
days no thats wrong six and god had it all
sussed till it came to people and he bloody well cocks it up
making the fella first   leaves him stark
bollock naked lying there playing with himself
cos theres bugger all else to do   then the silly sod
goes and makes him a woman   sets her down
on the grass and shes in the altogether too as me granny
would of   so   there they are nobody watchin what
they get up to and suddenly
                                        all hell let loose.

Anyway when miss Maunder said there was this
Big Bang it was bleedin obvious wasn't it
the universe was a bloody great row   fire
muck and bullets like all flyin every
which way   I thought that sounds more like it   at least
whoever thought of that knew which way was up   at least
when the dust began to settle and the stars came out
we could all have a bit of peace for five minutes while
the old buggers lay around sleeping it off and the women
could make a start   cleaning it up   so
I put that in me poem   only we had this

supply teacher said me sentences was crap
and it looked like Id never heard of full stops the rate
I was goin Id be on the scrap heap
hell in a handcart at 25
so I never wrote no more poems after that
and stopped lookin at the stars

The Monochrome Moon

Sifting footsand fools our screens with figment.
Pictures of grit, from the monochrome moon, would have us
    believe, once (maybe)
we stepped among stars, our petty footprint
treading giant parodies of moondance.

And forty years on, young minds I stuffed with promise
never saw the grotesque, technicolour,
    seven-league truth-leap,
over the program of a lover's dream.
Oil and coin have done for Shangri La. Yet,

before you strap your breast-bomb to a kiss,
weave me those stars, like roses, through your hair.
    Brave the pass.
Traverse our sable skies to stand and marvel,
silent, on some untrod moon of Darien.

Nativity

Bring out the stage blocks,
costume, manger, star;
old lines mumbled
on fresh lips, year on year.

Murdering innocents?
Look, oh look at the smiles!
This is the play. Already
they're learning their lines.

All stops for the concert.
Lessons on hold,
agonies over production,
tea going cold.

Even the landlord
is learning the song he must sing.
Look at the donkey!
Look at the face on the king!

Where are the bells?
Stage hand's away with a cough.
But listen. Already the shepherds
are getting first laughs.

Sir's on the lights.
The star in the hall roof is shining.
Somewhere, back of the classroom,
Mary is crying.

Kids In Port Patrick Harbour

Jumping off the end of a granite pier -
the show-off, me-first, me-as-well;
the nonchalant what's-it-all-about, and the one
who won't be shown up by his mates. One
with poems instead of courage, who waits
too long, but goes for it anyway. Last of all,
the small one, tiny brother, limbs like
tent-pole insects, whippersnapper, chipping at
the edges of rhyme, who's gonna do it just one time while
dad is watching.

And the girls.

Long, thin girls in wet, black suits.
Every bit as good as the boys
this one, and two with hair still way past their waists,
longing to take the plunge, not knowing,
would this be back to a world of street games,
smudged calculations in exercise books,
chewed nails and split ends? Or,
into deepwater murk, so green,
nothing to see till you're in there, over your head,
crabs and lobsters, concealed rocks and hazards,
maybe a pirate or two, with his treasure
and bones?

So two hold hands and leap out squealing,
out into air, into fast, clean air.
And velvet scoters, not really found in our region,
race like smutty black ambulances
to the very spot where they disappeared.

We Knew There Were Goats

Could tell by the smell,
that great mountain,
sure-footed stench,
that Jupiter scrambling,
dropped heap and urine
stain on each rock.
Deep in the gorge we met
two gentlemen
with neat, black beards.
Ignoring predilection,
peering closer, we
knew those polished pelts,
could sense wood-grain elegance,
antique patina coloured suave
in mountain air, an earthy palette
mixing myths of masterpiece.

But always, back to the smell.
Ripe smoke lingers in the cheese.
A reek of god and goat
we loathe to own, yet worship,
in spite of such bad press.
Alive to his moment,
old Gruff the Good Guy,
careless of bridges,
disturbing as bedtime,
stands above his fragile Billy,
daring the troll in me to come
too close and be caught
on the horn of his stink.

When Did Cows Become Vicious?

When I was young, cows were friendly,
hot, steamy, sweet-dung-smelling,
dollop-of-cow-pat-makers.
Lugubriously, they budged as you nudged
their fat, brown, black, white, overblown,
milk-maid-cushion bellies.

Walk the green track now, they amble
ever so slightly too quickly,
over a pock-marked body-land,
a plodged-up mire of clarts.

Now, they are eyeing us balefully.

Aye, that's the word.

Dark, come-hither eyes hot moist with purpose.
And of a sudden there's passion we never suspected,
pent up intensity, biding our passing.

How come we missed it?
How come we got it so wrong?
Is it something we've done to them,
chewing their sweet grass cud?

Now,

if we should cross the meadow,
one false move and we're down in the divots,

hard-pressed,

backs to the dry-stone wall,

up against it.

The Horses

There'd been no seven year war,
nor had I negotiated woods
that were beyond me. Simply came
to see the horses. I know they're here,
less than a mile from my front door,
frozen silent, always facing
a porthole of light in slabs of grey,
sentinels, if you will,
at the end of the tarmac way.

Stone and puddled tracks begin
a trodden grassway up to the woods
and moorland, seeded with fat, grey rocks.
Flank by flank, they root, hoof-splayed,
tails hung long as last year's willow-herb,
kissing, like courtesans, a first snow crust.
Wind-scoured, sandstone monuments
at January's gate, tired blankets
on a mind worn pale by my world,
scuffed to reveal my colour.

One foot, with infinite moment lifted,
set back firm in ploated, divot-scarred,
pooling mud and crushed turf.
Under a yoke of skies,
the weather balance trembles.
One jet-black eye (polished, funereal treasure)
tasting the world in a moon touch,
testing her temper,
watches a finger of wind write on grass,
waiting for mischief to pass.

Now, we all listen for one word on silence,
something under the paddock,
not stumbling rock, ice-mote trough,
uncoupled, ship-wrecked, railway wagon,
rook or double reek of horse –
under a dented, ramshackle bonnet,
the ancient gearing of our world has shifted.

Mr Hood's Farm, Bridlington 1956

Walking through wet, fermenting grass and dung,
her smell plunges me back, through a stinking
memory barn, to a five year self,
crouching under a beam of light,
throbbing with an ache of being me.

Hot-bodied beasts are hoofing reeking straw-stalls.
That light has to be morning. Crisp, white,
empty pages rustle . Someone
huge is helping the farmer draw,
with his mile-long ladle, out of a towering churn,

her warm thick milk. There, I drank deep as darkness,
fresh from her huge mother's body. I tasted
cowshed, grass and steaming decay.
Warm as the massive beat of her blood,
there I was, drinking the earth, and her byrey smell.

Her gorgeous stink travels everywhere with me, hot
as the presence behind, nudging me into the doorway.

Snow And Innocence

This phantom Jack is winter's joke,
shakes his frosty beard in midnight air –
vagabond in scarlet hood and cloak.

Leaping rooftops in the smoke
and steel of starlight when the moon's astir,
this phantom Jack is winter's joke.

Beneath a legendary oak
the villain finds another in his lair –
vagabond in scarlet hood and cloak.

Somewhere beyond the dark, a child
awoke mid-dream to steps upon the stair –
this, phantom Jack, is winter's joke.

So who believes in miracles? Folk
who shun grim symbols of the night declare
a vagabond in scarlet hood and cloak

is but a squeaking hinge, a broken
stair. Snow and innocence lie there.
Vagabond in scarlet hood and cloak –
this phantom Jack is winter's joke.

Shrapnel

Just when we thought it safe to be European,
    your child fist jarred.
Just when we thought man-gas stench was clearing,
    your razor-wire necklet.
Red pain, your small bone cinders glow,
while charcoal fingers frame a childish target.

Just when we thought alien potential fun,
    one black puppet
head, on a blast wall, bobs, like a boy undone.
    Confused by death, you trusted
our stranger's kiss. Now, rabbit blind,
your long neck rocks in a fire wind, torn and blasted.

Just when we thought deep myth a nursery tale,
    your curved, snake head
sways, poised with adam's poison. Feeling fails.
    Our mushroom outcast blossoms,
trailing a spear-wake, monster shade,
something we're never quite sure (to be fair) we believe in.

Just when we think we have your maiden prayer
    framed in plastic,
our goblin rises from ditches, foul as
    fair. Our cartoon nightmare
transubstantial, grit-thorn, fantastic,
burns our humdrum selves, like nature's whore.

Splash!

East Park

Lost in the wood,
come to a dark, brick tower,
beech-tree-screened,
deep in the park.

Pay your old, black penny
for the ride. Climb narrow,
zigzag, iron stairs.
The green moon crescent

lurks in her rough glass
cabin. There, amid
screams and silver swans,
summer is casting lots,

in beech crowns.
Boats on the lake
flit-flitting like skaters,
there, with silver pennies

tight in our fists,
we stare the green moon
deep between
her unrelenting eyes.

Ride the splash,
on cold rails, swerving
down to a lake
that found herself,

over the mud shelf,
way beyond Humber, Hull,
and a waste of curving,
out into clear, blue yonder.

Trawlers

St Romanus   Kingston Peridot   Ross Cleveland

Our City signature
in grey side-winders
snakes over a cold tide,
into the north.

Men, in their home-designer
ganseys, are translating bitterness
to hot, street-corner character,
frying the fog with flavour.

This, our legend, grained
as a monochrome pub crawl,
follows a dock rat,
scuttle-salute by the gate.

Three dancing dolphins
in Humber's mouth.
Three lone gulls pick
slick scraps from the mud.

Mud, thick as a dead dock mattress,
rocked on a memory tide.
Three jingling whispers
home on a following wind.

Their ice-furs cling white
as virgin kisses.
Death muffs grip the rigging,
garbed in cash splinters,

defeating the axe,
fanged as a pale wolf,
bear-coated, pawed
and savage.

These three flock,
like any ballad's adage,
legend's terrible
rule of three.

They limp home on Lupercal's
last wind, whispering their sermon
in tumbling, rolling, white-hot,
cap-sized syllables.

Hull, 1968

Gansey

Wool on five needles,
    clickety click.
All in the round, safe as houses,
    snicker snick nimble.
Finger, never a seam,
dream and remember
warm, blue-fibre knotwork,
feeding
ropework, boatwork,
tide, net, sea, wave and fish.

She knitted their dreams in a slip stitch,
    clickety click.
Pearled their plans in a fingerprint pattern of ridges,
    snicker snick nimble.
Her gansey might grace the deck
where she'd never step,
not if she valued his luck.

Her fingers were never,
    clickety click,
closer to his heart than,
    snicker snick nimble, when
she drew her designs upon him.
Woollen thread might thwart the ice.
Leave enough for a name letter,
    just in case.

Tide's Out

Hull and Humber mud glisten and gleam
in blubbery lump-fold frown.
Almost, you can hear the glooping.
Smell the salt-tang, brack wrack
fulminating on pier stock trunks.

Here, they would wash the horses,
Yorkshire muck and England sweat,
palmed off with grit. Now,
gulls populate and violate.
Sacred undulance foams volatile brown.

Eastward, the estuary spills her legend
slag, drawn on England's white-hot, seething iron.
Angry, cacophonous clatter boils,
draining a slough of illusion from green dale,
into an organ swell of Europe.

Misogyny

'Why are they burning the fields, mummy?
Why are they burning the hills?
What are those palls of white smoke flowering
over the wild wood fells?'

'It is summer they're burning with fire, my lovely,
blue days and golden gleams,
burning the halls of the bees of the morning,
dust on the old moon's sleeve.'

'What is that flame in shadow, mummy,
flickering mad as a hare?'
'The hazel thicket is blazing, my lovely,
the bones of our dreams are laid bare.'

'And what is the dance of fires, mummy,
I feel in the pit of my gut?'
'The bramble hedge is ablaze, my pretty,
your silks are all sackcloth and soot.

'They say it's because of the thorns, my daughter,
the razor, stiletto and crown.
They lie. It's our sisters they're burning
on the common, the meadow, the down.'

'And what is the sound that rattles, mother,
that frightens the bird in my lap?'
'They are blasting the heather and halls of the plover.
They think they will catch us like that.'

'What is the stench of darkness, mother,
filling my head with fear?
What is the bitter flavour of ash
that tastes like aloes and tears?'

‘They are burning a woman of straw, my dear,
heads full of shadow and gloom.
They are stoking her belly with buds of green flame,
her breast bone a kindled broom.’

‘Then why are my fingers so brightly, mother,
tracing an o in the air?’
‘They’re burning a hole in tomorrow, my child,
so no-one will know we’ve been here.’

And fields of the valley lay smoking. Rooks
made black rain shatter the skies.
Fox in the wind sniffed a wild boy flying
with Catherine wheels in his eyes.

Ballad of the Garden Crow

One morning of mist, in the smokes of October,
    new-minted frost on the trees,
a crow, with her feet on the wheelbarrow handle,
    sat watching worms in the breeze.

Adam went walking, in shadows and echoes,
    his feet were all covered in blood.
'What have you done with the children, our children?'
    asked Mary, as mild as a maid.

'I sent them to play in the webs of the attic
    with ribbons and rings and fine lace.'
But the crow, with her feet on the wheelbarrow handle,
    sniffed out the lie in his face.

Wind in the ruin blew ripples and rags,
    through dust on green weed and grey stone.
'Now what have you done with the children, our children?'
    asked Mary, so pale and alone.

'I sent them to school with a kiss and a promise,
    to dance, and build dreams in the sun.'
But the crow, with her feet on the wheelbarrow handle,
    smelt out the lie, like a gun.

Crazed are the windows, like eyes that are broken,
    looking on chaos and fear.
'Now what have you done with the children, our children?'
    asked Mary, her heart red, with tears.

'I sent them to bed with fire and a fever,'
    said Adam, his eyes grim as ice.
The crow, with her feet on the wheelbarrow handle,
    croaked at the bile in his voice.

Smoke curled from ashes and withering embers,
in cold wreathes of shadow and stain.
The bones of a city lay broken, a body
in fracture and pity and pain.

'Now what have you done with the children, our children?'
asked Mary, her eyes black as blood.
'Deeper than hell, we are buried so coldly,'
they answered her, bitter as God.

Now Mary, she wanders the earth in her ruin
and weeps for the laughter that died,
while Adam he cowers in webs of disaster,
beneath his illusion and lies.

And Mary shivers with pain, in her darkness,
for love that is broken and lost,
while the crow, with her feet on the wheelbarrow handle,
laments a bright glory that passed.

The Strangeness Of Oranges

Rode our bikes to Monument Bridge, except
it wasn't a bridge and the statue had gone.
Filled in the old Queen's Dock, shovelled in dross
while Wilberforce's towering phallus,
like the unfrequented moon, had moved. Still,
I wanted to peer from safe vantage, into
the maelstrom, wanted to see ghost-water
heaving and rutting, under a secret
garden bed. I wanted to know the blousy-breasted
three-masters, knocking like rickety, wormy four posters,
crack! on the weed-webbed wharfs.

Oh how I wanted the old Queen to be there!
Ghost rails bedded on cobbled quays. Ironway
wagons rumble tumbling doxies, roaring
shanty myths of old glories, half-learned, half-
remembered, smut-speck stories. There, would I
cycle into the waiting moon, keeping
my wheel just out of the groove, believing one
last tank engine might chuff round a corner,
shunting, clanking her coal-iron, black madrigal,
hauling before me all that signifies in dad's
Old Holborn tin of fog-flake stories.

Lingering, ready to cannon me back, is the smell –
rope, thick as a docker's leg, rank engine bowel,
tarpaulin, oilskin, coal-smoke, wet timber
dark as a pirate's jet heart, iron that rang
the century's great, cracked bell. Smell of fruit:
sweet pineapple, towering, play-castle rough crates,
erotic, intoxicating bananas,
wild fornication of citrus and tar. Somewhere,
the Sunday school, buttoned-up sharpness of lime
and lemon. In time, all monuments unwrinkle in the gut.
Onions fry myths in the belly.

Savour exotic, fairground fumbles
under the dark. A strangeness of oranges,
fragrant as desire, bridges, though no-one
can see through the whirlpool, the infinite, gentle
poles of our innocence.

Northumbrian Piper

No more dead lamb lumps to be coaxed
from a quivering ewe's hot body. Curlew
trills her flute, the shepherd piper
from the hills came down, came years ago;
grey hair fluttering, wind-combed wool on a fence,
eyes, like summer blue, fingering memory's note.
His deep round tongue, true as an old ram's horn,
modulated dialect of stone.

Joe Hutton the Piper's dead. My three year
education's ended. Bellows and bag
close round the belly for comfort; fingers dance
free on air, clean as a workman's whistle
timed to perfection. A crisp, dry wind,
cold off the moor's chest, sings like an angel thrush,
bursts from earth bladder, reeding raw fifths
under dancing stars on a drover's castle.

Spring reels on the river's ride, summer fruit
pudding of airs, moon's autumn jig, November
wind's lament and a heart-high hornpipe, all
stepped along the ranting hills. His music
beat the county heart green, tickling
tunes like trout below the Thrum
and now (like chicken pox) he's passed it on,
infecting generations with his song.

Bonny Bits

The old lead miners loved their bonny bits:
intricate webs,
miniature labyrinths under a Pennine wildness.
Microscopic, palace ornaments lit
their stone cold place. Staircase and balustrade mysteries, pinnacles,
minarets, ziggurats, roared to the worship of private gods.
Prism and spiral blueprint
carves a heart made land. Gritstone
mountain's DNA.

Crystal moments litter the levels. Erotic
geometry brought
goblin secrets from black tunnels into embarrassments
of light. Fabricated masterpieces leap
from the hammering, breaking, sifting and sieving the dead,
through bruised, arthritic fingers and thumbs. Over ground,
they labour, cold, carved
walnut, rosewood and maple,
in northern light,

fashion a cabinet under a woodman's blade.
Vine leaves and hippogriffs,
lions, dart-firing cupids, blaze on futures
fields. Versions of paradise showcase recalcitrant
passions. Fabulous passages articulate subterranean
pleasure. Chipped, cracked, hacked, gouged,
unspeakable vision, shovelling
birth, install stone legend
architecture of desire.

To cheat the grinding, shaking of the deads, under
a ceaseless turning
wheel, on days of celebration, he
steals light, ignites a bright passion candle
in despite of crow-black impotence. Flickering
in his cave, we are inheritors, beneficiaries
locked in a crystal fortress.
Resistance warriors share his obsession,
bonny creation.

Steelwork

Time harvest from earth's bodily fluids.
This image on a flat black screen, screams men
decanting fire, an engineering masterpiece.
Acrobats dangle from hawsers and pulleys.
Long, steel wands conjure coke oven magic.
Furnaces forge alchemical futures.

Supermen refine an iron pact. Cold, country death,
inflammable people of paper.
Darkness erupts in steel legend.
It takes a whole tribe, fair-bolting this myth.
Folk in thousands flock to their altars,
well-worn, brazen, sacrament scriptures.

Hieroglyphs of blood and ash
distil on sacred flesh, bone steles,
charcoal and fractured, lover souls.
A dark, apostle creed drags men from fields,
wasting women in a blood drudge,
spikes children on the spit.

This man, castrated by his tie,
this dark womb, teeming nuclear flux, they
shore up an ice-heap barricade.
And now, this dead-heart's age
reckons blood soil. Break faith. Break trust.
Break promise in the bowel.

Algorithms of the mind balance account and coin.
Erected palaces dodge coke-dust shades,
tar and acid sludge and scrap, unaware
earth moves. This mountain slides.
Slick manacles of grief. They fiddle, now,
in twisted wit, and dance their skeletons' gavotte.

Our Kids In The North

They're closing the Park School, built for the colliers' kids
on a green world's edge, close by wagon-way river,
smoke-stack sea, parched flower park.
Built for the bairns who bounced down wind of the pit,
sprouted mushroom promise, under an ashcloud.
A true proscenium curtain opened, where kids might
build their own reality, get their first laughs.

Old school bell, in the master's study, fattened
on top of the cabinet. Ring out the lazy peace.
Ring in the mal-adjusted,
rickety-rackety gods of old jingo.
Calculating machines, steel ranks of levers,
wait in place for a dithering, soft-finger crank,
to figure out the fatal fault of childhood.

And childhood danced and sang, where the fairground flickered.
Innocents claimed inheritance, out on the edge,
edge of town, of the pit land,
coalfield, minefield. Hordes of quarrelling,
laughing, murdering, giggling, thieving, squealing,
crying, screaming, smoking, squabbling, fornicating
souls, carved their star gems on bitumen.

All kept faith in a big rock, candy future, where
pits have porcelain baths to wash dirt clean of anger.
Hospital greyscale, charcoal company,
coal-dweller shades, nurse our black fever.
The broke-back, shot lung, dead finger tally
chalks up pony-soul memories on a pit-prop.
Failure of vision never undid such legions.

I Remember, I Remember

Backyard allotments,
pigeons and brass-band banners
on a wind-flash welfare.
Glittering eyes on a mission, gone.
Nor bang nor whimper, lamp in blindness,
never a song to burn through soul-cake,
stotty cake fairy buns.
Whipped up foam in a zinc bath Friday bubbling,
under the dead mandala,
pit wheel grinding.

Mine

Wor pit's a knacker job noo.
They've let the wattor in.
It seeps an' trickles doon faces
millions of ages aad cos
    the wheel's stopped,
    an' the pay's stopped,
    an' the tv winnat gan.

Wor hyem's a knacker job, noo.
They've let the wattor in.
The nights I got back pissed
an' blew up like a bomb
made cracks I cannat fix.
    An' the laughs went,
    an' the love's went,
    an' the cracked lives winnat mend.

Wor toon's a knacker job,
noo they've let the wattor in.
Thor's noot left after the flood.
They tried to plug the dyke
wi' aad pund notes.
Good for noot but lightin' fires.
Men on caad corners wi' black faces
an white starin' eyes like bastard minstrels.
    An the smoke's gan,
    an the hope's gan,
    an' the spirit winnat mend.

Wor young un's knackered noo, man –
they've let the wattor in.
You can see it in thor eyes, man,
infection's in the brain.
They dee noot, an they care noot.
What's to love, man, here, noo?
    Cos the tune's knack'd,
    an' the game's knack'd,
    an' history cannat mend.

Man! Sustainable growth is a bucket o' shit
when yer life an' yer soul is a bloody great pit.
Wor lass'l make buttons an frills for a cake.

Wor neighbours is shiftin'. Thor lad's on the take.
Sustainable growth is a bloody lang way.
Wor young un's bright future sustains noot the day.
    An' the heart's knack'd,
    an' the soul's knack'd,
    an' fine words winnat gan.

It's aall a knacker job noo, man.
They've let the wattor in.
An' they've made an arse o' that too cos
wattor ought to mend.
Wattor should clean an' bairns should thrive.
Wattor should keep leeks an'tetties an
me, an wor lass an' the young uns an whippet
an a strang place alive.

Mebbes it's aall to dee wi' the acid.

I divven'na but. Thor abandonin' millions
in tunnels wi' nee light, just
    slow
        rising
          deep
              wattor.

Poem written in 1990
Ashington Colliery 1867-1986
Ellington Colliery 1909-2005

His Poems

Grandad made his poems with a pick,
each bloody syllable bright anthracite.
Jowl and listen lad, perfect rhythm
taps across your face. All know just
how many hob-nail boots fit a line, while rhymes
for coal are plenty: foal and goal and dole.

Filled his tubs with stanzas, made you weep,
him and his marras scribbling come pay week,
plodgin through clarts to a black wheel stamped on heaven –
face of an angry god. Stone poem
prayers of light, so much dust you could taste
blood, fight, hate in his black soul's lung.

Carted off his god to a museum –
ticket and turnstile, coffee shop and I
will lift up mine eyes to the heap whence cometh beer
bread, profit and loss, pitch and toss.
And the pit shall preserve my going out, my coming
in and my going down, down, down

from fore shift to back shift and even for ever more.

Carted off his god to a museum but.
Knew where he was then. Filling his tubs with metaphors
grandad made his poems with a pick,
shored up the roof with angry words, set
fuse in similes and bitter jokes.
Expect me to write you love songs with nowt but a pencil?

Pass us a shovel.

An Eighties Lad

With apologies to John Betjeman

The light was on in the dining room,
the cat was in front of the hearth.
Dad was painting a skirting board.
Mum was having a bath, when
somebody came from out of town,
knocked on the door to greet them.
Told them the mortgage hadn't been paid
and the manager wanted to meet them.
Hurry along. Hurry along.
Have to be there by eleven.
Pay him a call at your local branch,
then hurry along to heaven.

The cat was up in the apple tree,
a sign was stuck in the yard.
Dad was pissed as a fart in a trance.
Mum was finding it hard, cos
someone had been with an envelope,
handed it over politely,
said they should sod off as soon as they could
cos the poor make the place look unsightly.
Hurry along. Hurry along.
It doesn't belong to you now.
Couldn't keep up with the folk at the front,
so there's bugger all else you can do now.

There isn't a soul on the rotten estate
who hasn't got hold of the yarn,
how him and the missus and both of the kids
are all dossin' down in a barn, cos
first they were after a couple of quid,
then they demanded a thousand.
Might as well ask for a star on a string,
when you've botched it, cocked up, blundered.
Hurry along. Hurry along
to the man in the suit and the grin now.
Pay him with water and bread and with blood.
It's time you were jackin' it in now.

A Study In Mathematics

We've added up the cost,
we've multiplied the bill,
subtracted from the best, till
there's nothing left to sell.

Next lesson is division.
Pay attention. Do your worst.
Separate the young and old,
the comfy and the cursed.

Divide vineyard and orchard
from the mined-out, clapped out north.
Divide the true believers,
rob the doubters of their worth.

Sever the blind from vision,
break the listener from the deaf.
Disseminate all union,
stop the speaker with his breath.

Stigmatise the joiner,
blue, green, yellow, red and hate.
Greyscale? Better sooner
Strike the black from white.

Divide the men and women.
Pitch all sheep against the goats.
Tear our mum from daughter.
Only count the ones who vote. Cos

we've added up the cost.
We've reached a firm conclusion.
Our scenario is host.
All that's left is long division.

The Woman In Suruc

Tall as a storm in the desert, swathed ankle to neck
in red and white check, she is the crimson ring
where armies manoeuvre.
They double-cross her chessboard, sacred quick,
wrangling for a chance to kill the king.

Good earth daughter, living geometry,
she inherits deep, atomic stars,
parabola joys.
No Euclid with his compass might deduce,
nor Moore, nor Epstein, imitate her worth.

Her printed scarf winds woman's hair
tight as a skull, black as the stain of tar.
Defending from desert
storms of obsession, veiled beauty's terror
flaunts riches with unsainted prayer.

Tight in her arms, the angry boy in black
stares over her shoulder. He sees what is coming.
Around her naked feet,
men squat on bedding rolls, flopped in a pack,
rags of outmoded clutter of possession.

All clarity is lost beyond her Form.
Definition shatters into pixels,
the arithmetics of care.
That black scrunch is a knot of angry counsel,
all but breaking her neck with a host of harms.

A Biblical Error

Why won't they hear me singing, mother?
What's a poor girl to do?
Only a man may sing to god child.
Woman's voice, taboo.

Where are my desk and my books, mother?
Why are my papers burning?
You have a womb and breasts, my beauty,
why must you hunger for learning?

But what have they done with my office, mother,
my tablet, my pager, my phone?
You frighten them with your spreadsheets, lovely.
Girls perform best in the home.

And why, when I go to the church and kneel,
do they tell me my prayers are obscene?
It's just that you've been bleeding, my treasure,
and that makes their temple unclean.

So who are these six bold men and true,
with lust like an iron bar?
What are they trying to do with me mother?
How did it get this far?

They are sons of the fathers of men, my child,
prophets, priests and kings,
hunters of flesh, lovers of steel.
Their embrace is a terrible thing.

So who's this driving our bus, mother,
our dark charabanc of the dead?
A man who's deaf to the hate in his heart,
a biblical error, by god.

All the policemen are turning away.
I'm dying as fast as I can.
They're afraid of a taint in the air, and a stain
on the uniform of man.

Your body was perfect for basting, my sweetheart,
for kitchens and baking and brine.
You had no place at the altar,
not with the bread and the wine.

Then I'll put on my purple shroud, mother,
my sacrament armour of blood,
and bathe myself in the terrible tears
of the Womanhood of God.

Children Without Voices

I wear this medal lightly in my brain,
stamped with hate, cast in the barrel of a Colt
    forty-five. Ribbon lines
flare blood fears at my fevered fault,
daring mysteries of math and mind.

I'll be no follower, no hidden slave,
behind the black. Scarlet, blue and gold
    explode my empty grave -
only the silence died. Songs unfolding
race through deserts, in a hunter's wave.

I'll paint my hands with henna for the wedding,
not with butterflies to dance on rain,
    or flowers for her bidding,
but with a calculus that measures change
and a formula for agents in the bleeding.

I was a child of paradise, whose river
ran with garbage souls, like a drain.
    I'll weep by no man's sewer,
shedding tears of impotence and rain
to irrigate his darkness like a lover.

I'll sing my song for children without voices.
I'll paint my hands for freedom to be wise.
    Fear the fall of darkness,
but fear of fear, that stills and petrifies,
won't murder me, nor love that kills in kindness.

My mind is sprung and locked on to their target
over the water. Who would fear the child,
    her life already forfeit?
Star-bound, she runs their ragged wild,
out-flies time with tesseracts and bullets.

Awards and fairies frame their grown-up wisdom
while gardens of verses riot in their market.

Cartoonist

Draw me a laughing Word I can chuckle at.
Draw me a joke with halo and wings
I can cackle at. In your great witness,
draw me a holy guffaw from your boots,
or the bile of my belly.

Draw me the rape of reverence. Draw me
a man with a beard, a cross and an ark
full of rainbows. Draw me pillars of good
intentions, columns of justice. Draw me
his engines of comic dominion.

Draw me a child whose head your pen can
explode like a diagram. Draw me a Laugh
I can strap to my wheels like a butterfly.
Draw me a heretic smile, whose punchline
squibs flame like Roman Candles.

Draw me a Laugh I can wear on my sleeve,
a Laugh I can crucify with
ridiculous nails. Draw me a Laugh
on the business end of a missile. Draw me
landmines of obscene hilarity.

Draw me a Laugh whose Name may never be
spoken. Draw, with lopped-off hand, a severed
head in absurd desert, fused and ticking,
underground. Draw me a laughing god whose
crimson tears boil as she weeps.

Paris, January 7th, 2015

Sooth

There was a time when truth came calling,
clattering the garden gate,
lifted the latch, rushed in courting,
  never late.

Was a time when truth came walking,
holding my hand beneath the trees,
shared a golden glass of beer,
  bright as you please.

Was a time when truth grew daring,
flying round the Ferris wheel,
holding lions in the forest
  by their tails.

Was a time, truth bowled me over,
stunned me with her winning ways,
captivated soul and body
  in amaze.

Was a time, truth played my love,
red as blood and piping hot,
rolled me in her arms. Lately,
  I forget.

I would have loved her like a maiden,
loved her mother's ample charms,
her old temptations, deeper than
  a host of harms.

Truth has shifted shape, like
old legend's monster on the fell,
fickle as ripe dragon-wealth,
  truth to tell.

Came a day, truth held me dying,
grey as an old, coal-seasoned fog,
left me by the river, lying
    dead as a log.

Truth, like printed, plastic heart valves,
digitally reproduced,
pixel-painted as you want her –
    new, or used.

Translating The Flesh

Radicalised at school
they read stuff on the internet.
Opened books. Guided by maverick teachers,
even took A Level courses, made
live poems, at home, in garden sheds.

She strapped unstable verses
under her breast. He left unattended
sonnets on the Metro, in shopping malls,
airport lounges the seedy, student
corners of pubs. They pressed the button,

exploding alphabetti spaghetti
ballads on buses. They fired rainbow
lyrics on visiting tourists. He flew
a drone poem over the Downing Street gardens
throwing the six o'clock news into meaningless

chaos. They had been reading all the wrong
poets. Or all the right poets, not
necessarily in the right collections.
They'd broken tradition. Wouldn't restrict
their study. Read pamphlets. Garish posters.

Websites! Poems dancing on Facebook
and Twitter. #amazelines.
It's rumoured they're stockpiling canister poems
to burst over towns and villages, showering
peaceable couplets. These leach

into your bloodstream. They believe,
when you swallow the Word,
it translates the flesh of innocents. Viral metaphors
multiply inside the swelling
atrium of your heart.

Beachcomber

Heart urchin – Spatangus purpureus

You came to my bed in the morning
from a room at the top of the stair.
Your sheen of silk was moonlight,
caught me asleep, unaware.
The room smelt of sherbet and liquorice,
ink stains, exams and a cat,
aunts' kisses and lost politicians –
the stains of our lives are like that.

You came with a kiss and a promise
and poems lodged under your breast
like smiles, or a dream, or an arrow.
All come with the wind, and cost.
You knew I would never retrieve them,
knew they were safe, beyond price.
No man would ever believe them,
no reader lend them a voice.

Two flotsam bodies, abandoned
by chance in a strange upper room
like weed, or the tail of a comet,
over a sad lagoon.
Drew my arm over your legend,
your painted skin wet as tar.
History carved, in shadow,
cracked lives on the stump of our star.

Leaving counterpane country,
we shook off our littoral crumbs
and, weaving a web of words, I missed
those urchin syllable songs –
tumour seeds endlessly burrowing
down through the sand of your breast.
I search in vain, at the turn of tide,
for a heart that was buried and lost.

And now my frail ghost scatters star lump
atoms over the sun, while,
under a lingering drench of oils,
your timeless colours run.

With A Pure Clear Light

Should I remind you of one winter's evening,
a scent of starlight pricked our upturned faces,
you would remember only a task well done.
We had escorted children to the theatre,
delivered charges safely to their homes.

Teaching in winter, a childish inspiration
fills the air like snowflakes. Should I now
recall that journey, to you it would be
tears of laughter left by the last flakes
falling on your face, nothing more.

Moments are steel, white snow, stainless,
fragrant as cherry blossom, tough as old
stars, gentle as the newly born.
Leaving the bus, you laughed, stepped into
snow. We set off, down the road to school,

walking in stillness through deep snow, sliding like children
since no-one could see us, and suddenly flying, surprised
by speed, brute rush of ourselves through night-ice,
skating on legendary ponds, hurtling
years of sooty footprints on the hearth.

Abandoned to the dash of glee, reckless, falling,
stumbling, catching, at ease in the first breath
of wonder, hands held against the spring –
both of us wanderers, deep in the silent wet.
The ghost of December moved secretly over us.

Should I remind you of those minutes, racing
the crack of stars, you would, perhaps, smile vaguely
disconcerted. Your windscreen cleared, we parted
for the moment, going our ways through winter –
you to your bright candles, and I to mine.

A Song For Lost Children

For Leanne, for Philippa

Summer should mean harvest bond,
apple, earth, onion scent,
fruitful chapel, rainbow's end,
school hall praising groaning weight.
Foison. None but a fool would use the word
these days. Anyway, it failed. Twice
picked up the phone. A broken bird,
moon cracked her news, *she died last night.*

Grief, our alchemist, can leaven
hearts, distil a wine of tares;
refiner's fire transforming dross,
philosopher's pearls to lodestar tears.
Our fellow selves, we trim like toys for a tree
or sew to a heel. Keep such twinkles hidden
deep, in pine wood corners, close to the heart,
where all but glows of sadness are forgotten.

Fail-stars close their eyes tonight,
lend light for centuries of grief.
We shall not stop the cradle, clear
the air, or smooth dishevelled sheets.
We can but wait, and blink, and murmur songs,
a clutch of wintry carols in the grey.
Like travellers' lanterns on a stranger's tree,
we'll ring the dark with candles round the clay.

In The Beginning

In the beginning were rivers, drains and dykes,
a thick, brown estuary ripe in smells.
Flat-earth farmland, drenched in lead-shot rains,
a crust of barn and dwelling in old brick,
    where we played war, on wasteland hills.

This was our hinterland of fogs and greys
beyond the lighthouse, boulder clay and gull.
Monochrome smoke stills Marvell's dogs,
a grammar school of reverential ways,
    where boys made empires in her walls.

Now, in borderland crag and stone,
curlew choirs, castle and island stills
and the angels' share, I'll unmask the hag
who stalks the foreshore, bed the queen of bones,
    who wrecked me in her shells.

The Old Gods

for Tom, and Thomas Enoch

Dad took me trainspotting, down to the railway,
iron-bellied titans steaming and roaring,
showed me the crossing, where I climbed on white gates,
rode them shut when the keeper wasn't looking.

Dad, granny told me, when he was a kid,
drew the innards of an engine, on a black school board.
Grew to love the big machines. Studied their anatomy,
knew the physiology of old, iron gods.

And he drew cathedrals, in pen and ink, for granny's walls,
wizard of the light and shade, master of the line.
Took me sketching chimneys, bridges, cooling towers,
taught me the better way to hold a tricky pen.

Then, there was the photo. His father, in a uniform,
(Faithful to the Empire, Alliance Souvenir).
Of course, I never knew him. He died long before me.
Century's ambassador. The play's pioneer.

I never got his story, just a tribute, from the war that broke
his body, threw him off the rails. Disemboweled time.
So flourish all your little flags, dark sea warships,
fragile images of planes, like small, white moths.

When we cleared the house out, found the other photo,
Grandad and his comrades, in the locomotive sheds.
Carte Postale from Belgium. Engineers, mascots,
saints and minor angels, tending engines of heaven.

Time to be star spotting, this side of the junction.
Catalogue the images, store them in a file.
Silver eyes that stare at me, far side of a century,
saw the seed of comets, in an old god's tail.

Trev

Had his own way of walking,
ambling rock and roll sideways,
a familiar carriage let loose on a branch line.
You knew his approach meant holidays, picnics, excursions.
Eyes, never still, darted like wrens through the undergrowth,
lighting on twigs, like a joke quite close to your nose,
held you in thrall as though you and the wren were both magic.

Wise fool, a voice rich in woodsmoke.
Counsellor, songs of a comic foil, words
assayed in a liquor of stars. Familiar master,
came striding through rushes and damp fields,
bearing fresh wood for our campfire.
Pursed lips frame that signal, new-every-morning
Welcome, in laughter. A new stage, progressing
our bold adventure.

Sage with a twinkle. Stand us a pint. Share us a moment,
handing humorous glory, over a stone font. Eyebrows aloft,
he rippled with gravity, pungent as greenwood smouldering.
That way of drawing his head back, cocked
at an angle of question, you knew he was about to deliver a gem -
just the right line for the song that was Trev,
sung in a fire's tale.

Still, we carry Trev round in our chuckles.
We know we can find him, down by the harbour,
watching the kids building daydreams,
messing about on the rocks. Best of all,
under a full moon, out in the dene,
Starlight Castle, built in the dark by mad Delaval –
dusk through to dawn, just to impress a lady –
Trev will be there, lending a hand.

Starlight Castle, Seaton Sluice, Northumberland. (Built by Sir Francis Delaval in 1750 after accepting a wager that he could not build a home for a lady friend in a day. The name comes from a local legend that it was started when the stars were shining and completed by daylight.

The Roundabout Man

Out of old, grey, corporation fog,
thicker than coal-smoke on council estate,
or fish stench on full tide, like the west wind's dog,
the roundabout man looms on the corner at top of street.

Can't place that power, not with a horse and cart.
No diesel or steam, his high-day harness,
must have been muscle-strap trenches thick,
cranked cold iron to spin kids alive in holiday darkness.

That vast horse shambled his carousel to a clop,
considered the snuffling lie of the land,
mumbled his nose-bag, steamed on his map,
whistled up change in his jangling, hay-scented, horse of a wind.

The boy, on a swing of light, took mother's hand,
ran helter-skelter, shiver and sway,
over the road and perilous land
from a three-cornered garden of fires, to the big wheel of his play.

And once he'd climbed that tower on terror's coast,
the antique mechanical rode him round.
Orbiting characters pegged out like ghosts
on a wire, turned the cabbage garden upside down.

Nor was it mother's hand in the hot, tar darkness,
gripped him tight as shed metal vice.
On trolley-bus wires, we twirled and tarnished,
danced on high, laughed and sang with a brave, new voice.

And still there yet, we tremble hand in hand,
top corner of yesterday, dark as life,
although we barely see him now,
or the shire beast, clopped to a halt and hot as grief.

But somewhere, the roundabout man still spins kids live.
Clutching the hope and bells of our harness,
we lose all thought. Tomorrow pales
to a foggy lamp, in the soul of an unremembered darkness.

The Dogtag Polka

Thomas Enoch Medd - WR/189127   Thomas Medd - 7668738

Fragments of identity,
documents of dignity,
tablets of infinity,
  brown, grey board.

Tokens of humanity,
slogans of obscenity,
notions of iniquity,
  dark as a turd.

Medals of modernity,
emblems of insanity,
rags of immortality,
  dragon hoard.

Slips of ingenuity,
dregs of imbecility,
legends of eternity,
  wings of broken birds.

Antidotes for jollity,
ciphers of absurdity,
jags of mediocrity,
  treasured, lost, ignored.

Labels of anxiety,
drugs of insincerity,
jigs of nonconformity,
incidents of piety
  lost for words.

Echoing uncertainty,
leaves of incredulity,
shading ambiguity,
shards of inhumanity,
  Eloise and Abelard.

In tobacco tins of infamy,
riddles of buffoonery,
these models of infirmity,
  marred, tarred pearls.

Supporter

I wore me tiger jersey
and me black and amber socks,
me football boots were gleaming,
there were creases in me shorts.

They picked the lad who stuttered,
the one whose glasses were held on with elastoplast.
They picked the little one with skinny legs
and Philip Green and Michael Rowntree
and they picked me last.

Me kit was never dirty
'cos I never dived in mud, never
made a sliding tackle, me
sliding tackle never would.

We stood there, in the drizzle,
making puddles on the grass.
They picked the lad with goose pimples
that prickled when we sat cross-legged in assembly.
They picked Alan Dennet, Alan Cleary
and they picked me last.

I played left back and wondered
how it was they seemed to know
who would run and wait, just where
the dumb ball ought to go. It was
me who made the banner,
'Come on Wivern', for the Cup, joined
the trip to City's ground, to see
the lads go striding up

to take the glory, I recorded,
on a counterpane of dreams.
I supported Roy and Leonard,
Kenny Curwen, Ian Dalby,
'cos they seemed to know
exactly where a boy was meant to go.
So it seems.

The Woodhorn Pit Explosion

1

The Great Coal Crow slept in his cage,
ventilation fan shut down.
(There was no report.)
Four men normally fed the fires round,
raising a steam of dragons, but
Woodhorn's fifty finest, by the page,
were away to the Somme, to saintliness and blood.

World, steam and weather's glass
were falling like a mother's dream.
Thirteen men,
bull-strong, from black bottom seam,
hauled up the incline steep as sin.
Stripped off (likely) sweating ripe as trash.
Sat down for a smoke. Cool off, with a grin.

Who knows which man, furthest inbye,
held a candle high, to scan
the dragon's belly?
Raised a light in the undercroft, to plan,
by his glim, where to set the new girder?
Who knew there was only one man bankside,
too much slag to shift, for love nor murder,

swamped in slurry too thick to pass?
And who knew that man, in chains, forgot
to set the fan?
August 14, 1916. Stop.
Sunday 6.45 a.m.
Who knew the seam was standing foul with gas?
They'd feed the flame of Flanders with the same.

2

Boom, said the drum, but it wasn't Kaiser Bill.
Woodhorn number 2, Low Main Seam.
Thirteen men
in the old crow's nest. Youngest, love's best dream,
21. Oldest, keeping the candle trim,
clickety-click. Thirteen men, whose drill
was keeping the world of night off our backs. Boom.

And the fall of the stone was 80 yards long.
One pharaoh, tombed in his pyramid,
coffin-sheen shroud,
raven, fit for the after-pit, slipped
graveward with his twilight pony.
And in wards, anthems of grief holding strong
to the tap of small coals and little money,

nurse virgins making shrines of holy
broken bodies, fell to the charm,
the anthracite kiss.
Out of the mouths of death, on wings of harm,
colliers' last lung rape,
lasses sewing gentle in lover clean sheets,
the devil gas leapt foul as an incubus.

Now, the pits are gone for tourist
parks, someone turns old
crow bones to song.
Look, Stranger, feel your century grow cold.
Grow roses in the hewer's wagon.
Love and anger flare like hidden gas,
while no-one has the wit to scare off dragons.

Postcard From Belgium

for Alfie

One photograph, they'd never know
I'd venerate its image. No message.
Only the silent, eloquent,
watchful grain of a dumb show.
Fifteen pals, familiars, grounding
him in the middle, hold my gaze.

Hammer, brace and dog. Always the dog,
man's best comforter, prince of the flock,
canine chancer caught mid-wag
at the front. All follow, cog,
clank and drum of purpose, wrought to keep
an iron carthorse on track.

All halt in muds of madness,
whispering gas. These bitter villanelles –
Flanders, Ieper, Somme – names, like all
good poems, ripe in gladness,
saying one thing, mean some ungodly
otherscape, some nest of ills.

Hammer, brace and dog keep the heart
beating. Odysseus hauls humanity
over the barbed and stinking swamp
of heroes. Wagons undermined,
ripe with sonnets, shore up clanking breaches
in the trench of obscenity.

One hundred years on from that cartridge
click, shutter clack, that snapped and trapped his soul
in an old tin box, kept
in the loft, maybe, in Dieppe, that
old tin shack is still there yet, and even
the dead rust rail is leeching red

iron pools, down through Europe's virgin
land. Though he died a score of springs before
I broke the lock, this father's hand
reaches to you, my grandson,
his mid-wag comforter, out of night,
one century of curious delight.

Letters From A Holocaust

O Herr, du meine Lippen zu öffnen;
und mein Mund shew her dein Lob.

Voices blow shades of old century fog, homely
epics in black and white. Their tongues
show forth kaleidoscopes, chorusing
luscious, binding hope. These are
their words. And we came listening down
from the hill in January dark.

Burns Night. But we heard fiercer verses
yet. Rain stotting off pavements, covering
fire. Words to flash in street-lamp flak.
Words to sting like nettle fistfuls,
prick hints of gas, scour the old years
clean from your skin, flare out on winter

wavelength. Words to strike a flash,
like Cupid's automatic dart.
Words settle in your belly like mum's plum duff.
And oh, how we listened, drunk in our season
silence, ears bleeding with tears. We came
to hear their messages from monochrome,

blood-red telegrams ringed on pigeon legs,
homing like peace, flown out of time
on a gospel. These, our actors, ladies
in fashion, hats on, wireless hope cabinets,
opened lips and their mouths showed forth
Nice, Vienna, Auschwitz and Rothbury.

Vergissmeinnicht

Lover-warm, salt flank, on a great, green
estuary shore. Belligerent rock,
her block church squats and stops
the always-afternoon sun.

Fisher-king cabins, on photogenic,
insect stilts, dip and sweep
their belly nets. Antique emplacement
creatures scoop their booms,

unburdening redemption seas.
And twelve boats nod, in the little channel,
tittle-tattle gossip on rickety rattle,
swollen, salt bloom decks, all summer through.

Round and round the petty streets,
white houses gather their painted skirts,
while saucy, gaudy, passion clock faces
chuckle at hollyhock familiars.

Each year, just here, the carousel
is winding summer's bobbin.
Children spin green-gold threads
on painted, wood-wonder steeds.

Dance their seasonal, rock-psalm pilgrimage.
Whisper their playtime secrets.
Tell *Vergissmeinnicht* tales
in a great, green, whale-basin of war.

Incident At The Menin Gate

From reconstruction in the square,
dancing carillon, war-drum poems
in gas, on shattered bones
and branches, to a barrel-vaulted
episode of names. You could
build this, in a shot, with kiddies' bricks:
outsized English church, too big for its boots,
final term exam room echoing
bang and shock, to petty playground
games grown out of hand. So we
perambulated in sun silence
shells, while the children came
running, scampering over the shadows,
scrambling, stumbling up steps, chasing
wildly round unguarded corners.

Some fat, old ruler nearly called for
decorum. This was over the top.
But then, one small boy, lost in a sea
of troubled names and faces, shouted,
frightened, panicked maybe.

'Papa!'

And the century fell away.
The child's cry thrilled above twisted,
barbed remains of foolishness.
And death-white stone
and blood-red brick dissolved
in Flanders mist and I shrank back,
cowered under a mess of might-have-been,
mortified I might have hindered
the majesty and burning
        of the child's cry.

Defenestration – October In Prague

Always expecting Kafka, Prague, for me,
metamorphosed middle Europe
history to the sacred carol dance.
Teenage nightmare tanks and comic bombs
in midnight square, thousands of candled faces
burning hope, a schoolmaster's frightful joke
to remember the French for window, hurled
confusions of accents from high landings,
to shatter porcelain poems and bones,
on golden lanes.

Jostling for song space, potfuls of innocence
painted Lennon's face in house-high splendour
(walrus and submarine).
Charles, on a fairytale bridge, pirouettes
in metres of jazz. Smetana storms
the Rudolfinum, burnished in golden
autumn's image. Drink a half litre
of Radegast Pilsner in Wenceslas Square.
Marvel (elsewhere) the magic clock
whose maker (according to story) was blinded.
Savour all dumpling textures and flavours,
just like moments of Prague, in late-season
sun, before a deep and crisp and even,
winter story lays hold on your heart.

And as I share, with you, these memory lanes,
over the phone, I hear, or
think, or dream (perhaps) the click of someone
listening on our line. Already, I can hear
the lies (already) they may be
telling about us. *Život je hořký:*
Bohudík.

Radegast *is a Czech beer named after a god. Stemming from the name is the slogan: "*Život je hořký: Bohudík*"*[1]*, which translates "Life is bitter: Thank God"*

1. Zheevot yay horzhkee: Bohoodik.

The Molecatcher's Gibbet

Black jet princes, twenty-six aristocrats,
each a hand-span slap on the year's new face,
hang all arse-down on a barbed fence.
Their nuclear option jest of execution
    waggles and warns.

We're out to get vermin, warm in their moleskin
cuddles. Happy to be beguiled in green willow,
we venture truth beyond winter,
January underworld, encountering
    diamond cadaver

occlusions, in chiselled violence. Fifty-two
tiny paws, digger claws, rake hard, white, scoured sky,
ripping a last, rebellious
gash, a furious stroke over wasted land,
    in cold, thrashed sunlight.

One artist daub, open-mouth, vermilion,
screams in time, bare, needle-tooth snarl. Angry, ivory
pain. Fine-tooled, plastic miniatures
I never knew were there, comb air for resistance. Five
    inches underground,

soot-berries are dreaming their dark. And what's it for,
this country Tyburn? Who will see our Lordenshaw
gallows? Will it be moles?
Will they know velvet comrades, unpicked by wind crow,
    strung on a wire?

Choose Your Palette

Childhood was greyscale, all our records
black and white. Documentation,
newspaper, TV, nation, pictures,
textbook photos. Diagrams explode
process, dots before pixels.
Monochrome shades paint plus and minus.

Celebrity posed greyscale glamour.
If there was colour, we couldn't
afford it. Monochrome is in the bone.
Ghetto walls ring memory fragments,
family groups, holiday
stare, familiar faces my shadow touches.

Whispering, town alley entrances,
snickets, uniform darknesses
fade out of half-tone fog. No-one predicted
parades of stiff-legged parody. There,
in my personal black and white, even
now, if it's monochrome, it must be me.

Feels like my grey soot-fall from brick chimneys,
tastes like mine. Leaders and generals
click to their greyscale orders. Lines
of people pour from doorways, tickertape
movement records, traffic
and causes. Children with uncertain faces,

grey coats too big for them. Suitcases
litter the platform. This monstrous
shibboleth shuffles behind us.
Grit-ash clings under fingernails. Nostalgia
makes me own it like a dog,
wagging his tail, slobbering over the colour box.

Wintersong

My lady, with her yellow hair
and crimson coat of threads and patches,
leading her troop of clowns and catches,
danced along the wintry air.

She leapt upon our little stage,
and all the children at her feet
chuckled through sharp hail and sleet,
like ciphers on an antique page.

Through every scene, I played the fool,
December man in cloak and cups,
a shadow on the frosty steps,
a ghost of misremembered yule.

Our lantern shone. My lady laughed,
danced to the rhythm of an old guitar.
And while we practised to adore,
I heard my heart unbend at last.

Through laughter, in the frosty air,
through words of wonderment and bells,
I caught, before the shadows fell,
my lady with the golden hair.

Folly

Oh! I could lead you astray, if only a little way
out of town, bracken and bent, to the oldest fat
folly in the county.
Simpering, sultry pink foxgloves nod, open-mouthed, in a heart-stop
still.
Briars embrace in song each green top hedge, dilly-dilly,
come to the dance.
Cocksfoot is clubbing the hot-dew summer.
Filigree tracery, green-lace cow parsley is flaunting
her bodice and morning
ripe as a land girl, frequented by saucy, brown butterflies.
There's hot bee buzz, gold
lichen fizz on bed stone passion.

Last, thin, may shreds of a pale gown dazzle yet. Damp-full bright
berries are blazing and roaring their morning bronze.
Lean, for a sweeter view,
into the wormwood-silver stink and brushed-up, pale, land-fell of
hedge eggs.
Dodge green leather dock straps. Ignore grumble-rumbling,
dead hogweed choirs.
In a green gloom of fern bank shades, pantomime characters
frolic in ditches. Butchers, plumbers, teachers and vicars
park their lustful, dark dreams
where a bad-tempered protest of rag-rooks cranks the loud ratchet.
Cross water, where signal
butter flags wave, by the last cottage.

Grass and elder weed-crowned, wind-blasted smooth as a baby's kiss,
round as a dead liner's funnel; tower door tight
as a treasury purse
putting stop to all vagrant dreamers, vandal warriors, hospital
lovers inside for illicit progression of sins.
Sandstone learners
boast a regiment flayed smooth by curriculum.
Labourers forged this Babel mockery, this holy man's
black error beautiful.
He scored his town project in universal blood, that he, by
lent workers' coin, might
see the engineering mind of god.

Trinket

So, I bring you, late as lone, to this hollow hearth-place; earth and graven
stone lump-lifted, set down by design, by love's ease, here.
Green floor remembers well her
step dance, her whispering, lark-song foot-fall, peat-burn music, windchanter
piping a stranger's melody, homing heart-wise.
Her shadow bower,
long and far from our sober house beyond the river,
soothes under her silent, long caress. Eastward, motionless,
falls the sea. Notionless
frozen, wind-white alien turbines tread her soft horizon
grass, till the wind-rush,
canoodling hum sings with engines.

We share moor monuments with fox and adder on the margins.
Nibbling sheep nudge deer dung heaps in her gentle hearth
place here. Neighbouring
hills haunt fellow memories like grey-fell fox-holes. Concrete dug-outs
impart a bed-time, nightmare narrative line-spike
Forgotten camps cling
to the ring-cup shell of a life-long fort in the wild.
Chirrup and whistle and wheatear chack, raw rook croak,
dead-tap, rattle-time codes
in legion chaos. Rain riddles earth on a border fence, where
rolling north wind tales
twitter like musical autumn leaves.

I might offer you home in her visionary moment,
calm, beyond the tyrant shadow of an old firm
tracked here in rucksack and rhyme
avoiding the baggy-trousered crow, black weather spot on a dark sky
hunched on a dead limb, pecking his unforgiving fleas.
Hope tells her dream,
her overwhelming, meadowsweet love-scent in a ditch
outranking purple cranesbill, dead strictures of sinister
woundwort, wormwood. True love
trinket maybe. Abandoned, wayside treasure, tumbled or no.
Let it go lost,
this fallen nip-tight strangle, round a dead lamb's tail.

Have A Poem For Your Birthday

for Jill

Not a wild, drunken rant of a poem
full of raucous, chiming rhyme
and pedantic rhythm,
nor yet a pale, beige sweater of a poem
with dainty feet and tasteful endings. No.
Make this a full-bodied, 50 candle power poem,
chocolate-fuelled, bursting with possibilities;
a poem to fire rockets (or puddings)
and roast chestnuts.

Have a fish-and-chip supper of a poem
washed down disgracefully with golden wine.

Have yourself a poem full of boys who tell stories
and come home covered in mud; of girls
who climb trees full of mischief in dresses that
never stay white.

Have an old-fashioned forest of a poem
where there are dragons,
a glacier-crested mountain of a poem
where there are unicorns;
in midwinter half-light, have on the house
a sun-scorched beach of a poem
where the strand line is littered with
metaphor cocktails.

And as your birthday closes,
have yourself a dream of a poem
where your unsteady world
puts itself right
on a higgledy-piggledy keel.
January will turn her page,
        pick up a new pen
                and set about making
                        stories in magic ink.

Early Gardening

You shouldn't dig when clay sticks to your boots,
the year's too young.
Long weeks of wet and slow frost-melt imply
a dissolution of drifts.
Winter fires warm your draggling drench
and still cloy
stays your step, on a drunk field.

Slick, brown earth-arms clamp your ankles.
Slow, fat feet
are mud-wrestlers, gliding down on polished brown,
wet as an open body.
Our stumbling staggers bruise, where slated ground
is glazed to a shine.

Striding through my garden, you melt frost,
tendering cold ground
till surface is claggy as underdone cake.
I've been here
since morning, tramping through clarts that cling to my soles
by the inch. Soon,
half the scripted earth will stick to my feet. I'll be
walking too close to the sun.

A Way Through The Woods

You should have been with me today,
not for the quicksilver birchwood veins, laced across April blue,
nor for pink opal, long-tailed singers, jeweling the parchment bough,
but for a hot sun sit on the boundary stone
and a massive, windblown rootplate, black as winter.

You should have been with me, not
for the gatepost-hinge-creak pheasant, but the hush and hum of traffic,
furtive as unseen bees. Not for the nid-nod, see-saw chiffchaff,
piccolo-dazzling wren or pigeon rumba,
but for deep holly shadows, bitter with prickles.

We should have climbed these woods
together, not for the spiralling children's schoolyard voices, beyond
beech stumps felled with their ghost swings, nor for trembling
rhododendron
leaves bibbling with whispers, but for the rank and file of veterans,
grey as infantry, shell-shocked and terrible, reaching twig fingers
up to the rattle of geese, boot-crunch,
beechnut crackle-popping like innocent mornings.

We should have been, not for the quack
and waddle of duck in the sheep field staggered with cattle, horns
curving an auroch's myth, but for the heavy thump,
thump of your heart in your ears and a glittering anklet
snail trail. These are the wildwood paths

we should have taken, not for
rust-red stands of pines, blousy with needles, nor the remorseless
tock of the woodpecker, but for the lichen- and lime-stained, air-
moulded,
water-grooved, gouged, cupped and rain-bowled
rock where a lady from the town feeds the squirrels.

These would have been our ways,
not for the flap dance of butterfly tapestry, semaphore summer
peacocks, dark as velvet concerto notes on a high cloud,
but for the sake of sewing a second shadow
and half moon hoof prints in black earth.

Children, cars and chaffinches
whisper, cry, play wars and bumble bees bum. This should have been

our way through woods, not for the workman-whistling blackbird's
cheek
but for the fat, grey rock where mischief and lovers
carved their names in 1935.

We should have shared this day,
not for the flickering songthrush laughter, new spring cover of bilberry
but for the old, arthritic squeak of the kissing gate, the bog
source of a little stream, whose still, black pools are dancing with
skaters.
Not for the alien, folded, brow-curved, goggle-eyed, mushrooming
rock like a boil
erupting from subterranean fables, not for a backward
vision to woodland wild, but a bend in the track.

And it would have been this way,
but for a change in the wind, a turn of air to a hazy horizon,
elf-hills, legend thick. We should have crossed this telegraph
tramway,
insulators brimming like summer pudding, crossed
this long-ignored, forgotten boundary – fifteen twisted hawthorns,
four long dead, snapped off, one horizontal, leaning into the east,
this dry-stone wall, ten courses in its day, now two,
half its length, a single step. Hole-gape
blown wide as time.

I would have taken you
over sand-soft turf, to a low, barbed fence. Look there –
a silver lake, thought-still in afternoon sun, barely
ripple notes, in spite of a cooling breeze. And I would have brought
you
down again – not by the sorrowing magpie's single flight,
nor, out of sight, the harlequin-jesting jay, but by the fiery,
crackling, lemony, sharp as sherbet gorse bush, golden green as time.
And the fond, deserted, perfumed garden of bonfires.

Talisman

Here is the house I promised, one day, I would build for you.
Here's the door we should never have found, at the end of the
avenue,
a thing of crisp words and promises kept too late for you
that only a poet, with no sense of timing, could write for you.

Pause in the hall by the stair, there's time and a place for you
and music. The garden's awash with honeydew.
Through a door in the lines, a room full of senses on fire for you.
Take tea. Embers will cool. Come morning, a wind sweeps the
residue.

A kitchen of sonnets and sweetmeats, full cupboards of song for
you.
Gin and lime in the garden. It's summer, throw rhyme on the
barbecue.
Upstairs, in the bathroom, a shower to rinse clauses clean for you.
Old stanzas run clear. Can you hear what the metaphor means for
you?

In the bedroom, ballads of darkness and epics of dream for you,
and a curtain to hold back the night, so your day won't be
misconstrued.
This room full of books is unreal, and yet always meant for you,
Here in grey dust, is the ghost of a line someone sent for you.

In the cellar, wine, beer and laughter of bright girls and boys for
you,
a dusty collection of memory, and old children's toys for you.
I could sleep in the attic, a rug on the boards, to watch over you.
The sparrows are no trouble. Trust me. Our banter won't bother
you.

Of course, I was never there. You're quite safe. It was all for you.
I'll just bury these verses, for luck, underneath the front step for
you.

Genesis

Greatest Villain of our age were Marx –
Karl or Groucho? Who cares, come the dawn?
Blast revolution boy! Send in the Quarks!

Sound trumpets! Pop the daddiest of corks!
Serve wines of genesis on heaven's lawn.
Greatest Villain of our age were Marx.

A universe in thrall to cosmic clerks
who calculate the chance of being born?
Blast revolution boy! Send in the Quarks.

Somewhere beyond the party line there barks
an old dog fox who prophesies the moon;
Greatest villain of our age was Marx.

Unable to believe the future works,
or see how levers of an age grow worn?
Blast revolution boy - send in the Quarks.

Ancient and modern - conjuring the dark's
a dodgy chemistry, come sense or charm.
Greatest Villain of our age were Marx –
blast revolution, boy, send in the Quarks.

Where There Are Tesseracts

Imagine a point. Let it be perfect,
immeasurable. Nor height nor length,
depth nor width, heaven nor hell.
No journey, no horizon. In silent,
infinite stillness, let your point be.

Now, move. Choose wisely
direction of travel, distance, be certain.
Determine trajectory, move to your destination.
Finger space, one single unit.
Create the perfect line, begin and end.

Wait for dust to settle, then
move your line one heartbeat, just the right
angle to itself. Create
a perfect square. All ninety, bewitching
moments. Such perfection, like peace,
is impossible yet, we fondly discuss
its diagonal. Square root of two. Something which
cannot exist, for it cannot be measured.

Take your square. Hold it to the light.
Delight in exquisite impossibilities.
Clean-ness of corners. Secure lines.
Lack of duplicity. Move your square.
Let it glide. Let it slide over a third
sea of infinite dimension, where
the mind wallows in sunlight and fresh rain.
Delight in the birth of cockle-shell beauty.
Let your square travel one unit, a perfect
attitude to itself. Create a cube.
Balance your cube on a pinhead. All angles ninety,
lines one brain trace, squares perfected. Perfect.

Such perfection, like truth, is impossible. Yet,
we unflinchingly trace his diagonal.
Square root of three. A policy, like freedom,
that cannot exist, for it cannot be measured.
Yet, you see your cube blazing, scintillating,
dancing naked over the waves,
pirouetting in madness over the shoreline,
into the forests and fields and woodland shires.

I believe nothing which cannot be measured,
(diagonals of peace and truth
and freedom) can exist. Nevertheless,
it is time. Move your cube. Move it one,
single, finger's kiss. Translate this
precious manifestation,
directions that cannot exist. Be gentle.
Such impossibilities are fragile.
Keep them safe, by your heart. Go with them
into the unknown. Move your cube
just the right angle to length and breadth and depth
all at once, to a place you can only imagine.
Let it be love.

Thus, create your perfect tesseract.
Corners and lines, faces and cubes
perfected. Perfect. Like peace and truth,
freedom and love, your tesseract can not exist,
although we debate her diagonals.

Believe in your point, your line of travel.
Be sure of direction and distance. You
will not get lost on a road that cannot exist
to a place like memory and hope.
Travel in dreams, where there are tesseracts.
Take my hand, to a place we were not meant to go,
where infinite impossibilities dance on a pin,
round laughter lines in your mind's eye.

Searching For Nirvana

I had a little spaceship,
everywhere I flew,
the monsters I encountered
resembled me and you.

People in their thousands
came to welcome me,
with planetary wonders
and buttered scones for tea.

Star silk, sun spice,
jewels of the moon -
a universe of sweetmeats
and one plastic spoon.

I had a little spaceship,
everywhere I flew,
babies in their cradles
reminded me of you.

I bought a little nut tree,
nothing would it bear
but silver for your images
and gold for your hair.

So I skipped across the galaxy,
by poem, moon and tree.
All the shadows in the air
couldn't catch me.

Washing The Dishes

Someone before you has probably piled the sink,
pots and pans, blood-slime fragments,
recently dead Bolognese,
cold, thick water.
Lift everything out, like poo-caked nappy, pregnant vomit.
Stack on one side.

Run scalding water. Fill up the bowl. Add apple
fragrance, or lavender. Delight
in the dance of the bubble. Start
with the cleanest.
Maybe you shared a glass of wine. Find the print of her lips.
Gently erase,

like blood from a child's graze. Probably best to rinse
glasses – the rest may safely
drain dry in the wholesome
emptiness
of your well-planned kitchen. Tea-plates, cups and saucers
lightly soiled need

little rubbing. Dinner plates, cutlery require
firm treatment. Always remember,
fork and spoon have been in her mouth.
Handle with care.
Finally, preparation vessels. Carefully wipe
your cloth in curves,

creases, ensure the smallest fragment dislodges,
sinks in your grey water.
Remember, always avoid
too much abrasion.
You may wish to repeat the occasion, new wine, richer
sauce, perhaps.

Same lips, different messages.

Trust Me, I'm A Poem

When I touch you, there will be no pain
only grass stains and a little tingling.

When I hold your hand, there will be no applause.
My palm will be warm not sweaty and the arthritis will have gone.

When I sing songs, no-one will weep. Guitar strings will jingle
like ancient harps. Ringing in your ears will fade into white
silence,
and you will sleep.

When I look at you, my words will shiver into 13 new forms of
ambiguity.
My lines will trip over their own feet, to dance with bees.

When you look at me, darkness will cover the face of the earth,
but only till morning.

When you taste me, it will be beef and carrots, haddock and thick cut
chips,
black pudding and bacon, pink lamb's liver in a sauce from
Cognac.
It will be dumplings and sauerkraut and curry and elderflower
wine.
Or ginger beer.

When we fight, there will be stars and lightning. When we curse and
swear
There will be thunder only trhe gods can forge, but always
after the storm will be rainbows.

When I walk beside you, the path will be paved with gold safe as
houses.
And houses will throw wide their doors tonight, in a heartbeat

When I lie with you, there will be metaphors. Stillness in hurricanes,
fire in snow, trust in great fear and, come morning, under the bed,
one vast, unfathomable trunk of memory.

When I fight for you, nations will throw down their borders. There
will be
no more war, no more watch-towers, no more barbed wire,
trenches

or missiles. There will be only a mutual sharing of water. When I
show you Prague, there will be jazz on the Charles Bridge.
In Norway, glaciers will reach out their paws like a wolverine.
In Africa, symbols will halt in the face of elephant, lion
and smoke that thunders.

When I bring you a button, there will be a new dress.
When I bring chocolate, there will be sticky fingers and stained
lips.
When I bring a ring too many possibilities let's not be silly but
when I bring you a rough, quartz pebble that looks
nothing on the outside, there will be glitter and crystal
and, best of all, seasides.

When I walk away, there will be no sadness, only a new page,
silence under the sun, a taste of honey, hint of roses and a child
with eyes like sapphires. You will lie down in a field with your
book,
and when you rise, your form will be printed on cloths of gold.
There will be stains of grass on your dress, and a little
tingling.

Draw The Curtains

The green curtains.
Write them shut, against silence
and an invasion of dark.
Tell them,
neatly pleated ,
in folds every fifteen whispers,
a pattern of words
against fear
of chaos.

Sing me the song of green curtains
you made for our last home,
brought with us, folded,
like my lust, in a tea-chest,
inside an old van.
Tell me the rhyme of curtains you took out,
shook out stale, musty words for an airing,
to hang on a line in our garden,
where neighbours might see.

Make me
a psalm of green curtains,
ironed smooth as your skin,
held warm in sun's light,
folded around me,
against the dark,
and fear of chaos.

Under Glass

Outside rain drench teems with common sense,
we are on the Italian terrace,
    sheltering under glass.
Reality is a well-trimmed garden.
To all intent and whisper, we stand,
fellow travellers under a priestly pardon.

Took out your phone, not to call
from lately-lacquered, Victorian,
    florid iron work,
but to snap the virgin robin shrugging
shards of shell. And falling still,
fire ash drops in bling, from webbing and wings.

Winter plans well-founded. Family visit.
Christmas purchase. Children worship.
    In two cars we travel,
taking one direction home,
daring to hope and trust the weather's
ancient tendency to vanquish harm.

Chamber Music

All the while our music plays,
dance the long live days away.
When the piper stalls his breath,
steal a chair, steer off death.

Now the fiddler bows her string,
rant and make the welkin ring.
When the trumpet winds his horn
spring's a laugh on slim, green corn.

While the harp strings leap and flame,
burn the straw, heal the lame.
As the cymbal rings and freezes
echo stings, death comes easy.

For the dark bassoon advances,
starlight turns, legend lances.
Tap on winter's timbrel skin.
Kiss and tell the lovers' hymn.

So, round the house our music plays,
weep these carolling days away.

You

You are the snow that burns the coal,
you are a fever to calm the soul.
You are a star that falls by day,
you are dark that lights the way.
You are music to still the wind,
perfume that scratches the mind.
You are a taste of hope in the lungs,
silence that speaks in tongues.
You are the voice of oysters and pearls,
you are a poem that stretches and curls,
rhyme that shivers and giggles,
a line that wanders and wriggles.
You are a song to listen on sadness.
You are a word to write on madness.

Emailing Aphrodite

Our emails to each other are full of light and laughter
a comedy of manners, froth of word on water.
One switch-click in the memory, one whisper in the ether
is a flickering of starlight, where shape and shadow gather.
Our virtual engagement is more than ring or letter,
a web of breath and rumour, an intimate connection.
A murmur of mortality thrills like a note in the chorus.
The truffle predilection I shared with young Adonis
was cause for consternation, but you sent a patch to cure it,
restoring registry and life, rebooting faith and habit.
E-fingers on the keyboard, e-coals upon my tongue
unleash a storm of madness that rattles in my lung.
E-figures dredged from chaos stand on a shelf of dreams,
wreathed in summer tresses, like ancient themes.
So I send you squibs and fragments, you touch my lip with sparkles.
My songs are wrapped in laver bread. You spin me lines like cockles.
But meet me in the office, by desk or water cooler,
or tired outdated server – it's business as usual.
While midnight on my keyboard is tapping indiscretions
that sing like minor tragedies of passions and possessions,
our silicon endearments forge an ancient application,
generate a text of love, memory and ambition.
So my songs of wine and playtime go windily and lightly
round children in the shadows, when I email Aphrodite.

Songs Of The Healer

For yours are the songs of a healer,
sharp as morning dew;
yours are verses high and clear,
swallow song and a weather's tear,
hair and hope askew;
a wheel of something new
  that spins and spools.

For yours are the tales of a healer,
deep as dragon sheen,
bright as a diamond, cut on the sly
with a sliver of ice from African sky,
full of sun like Burgundy wine;
a lode of light down the line,
  trinkets and fools.

For yours are the hands of a healer
marking my palm with prayer,
pressing my lips with wintry fire,
burning symptoms of faith and desire
at the foot of a broken stair.
And nobody knew you were there,
  with your flagon of souls.

For yours is the breath of a healer,
saving life with a kiss,
prince or pauper,
Jupiter's daughter
dancing, more or less,
in yesterday's wedding dress,
  with your bait box of jewels.

For you have the look of a healer
caught in a sideways glance
offstage, act three, too young for me,
too soon for old mother tree,
too long for the autumn dance.
You brought me laughter, once,
  in a balsam of spoils.

Note: in the north-east, bait *= packed lunch*

The Midnight Crossing Keeper

October1969, somewhere on the A63

A hard journey I made of it,
leaving the main road utterly
the wrong place, too far south;
accepting all the wrong lifts,
dropped in some pretty mad spots.
And my mate's voice, over a pint,
chuckling this was all folly.
A darkening story. Started out
in light, soon I guessed I'd be travelling
all night, sleeping on verges, perhaps.

Pitch dark, but for the legendary stars,
heathen-looking elms on a winter skyline;
flat land drained by dyke and fleet, steeped in
someone else's language. And by the time
I stumbled on the level crossing, God
I was shattered! Totally misjudged distances
and times between two rivers, yesterdays' kisses,
eyes through a smeared screen.

He came out, found me lost on the road, miles
from anything like a pub or a girl, wandering
out of the dark. Took me in the signal box
loud with light, a fairground palace of brilliants.
Thermos tea, hot, dark, sweet as a drug,
jammed paper cork stopper, tight as a vaguely illicit
hug. And a long, old railway, leather bench,
draped in a rug where I could have slept but
where was I going? A train was due. He'd close
the gates too soon, maybe we'd catch us a wagon
bound for the docks. He wouldn't refuse. The guy
took me all the way, well Hopewell Road end,
twenty-five moments from home.

All this was a long time ago, I remember;
probably dead now, my crossing keeper.
I wonder though, was I unique, or did he
often lift up wanderers out of the dark,
give them his tea and a bed and did he
remember? Or is it just me? Too far down
the wrong road, too many stops, poor beginnings?

I would be glad of another lift now, hoping
for words to recall how, just when you think
you're up the creek, you come to a crossing and
up pops the signalman.

Love Song

Hope of fish and chips beside the seaside,
taste of nut brown ale on autumn nights,
honeydew's excess in summer moonlight
    and snowball fights.

Onion sizzle in a neighbour's kitchen,
fragrant pavement under new spring rain,
perfume in a kiss I still remember
    again and again.

The long silk scarf that rippled back behind you,
an oak tree's bark beneath your finger tips,
shower pin pricks on your body waking
    and tulip lips.

That old back gate that crashed with you arriving,
guitar strings picking dreams along the wire,
a voice beyond the pale, whose notes I treasure,
    words on fire.

Songs we made that telegraph the moment,
your murmur in the starlight of a word.
My senses fail to call, to catch, to keep you,
    now all is absurd.

Your many persons on the boards beside me,
your shadow in the footlight rings,
your hair, your eyes, your hand beneath my fingers,
    a glimpse of wings.

Midsummer Weddings

Rabbits riot over clay-parch-dry, play-park-dry, priest-parchment
droughted, rhubarb cordial, hay-dry lawns.
Swift-gossip blackfly-freckle, stipple-blue gossamer thread-needle
tight
morning gasping
rattles brass church door keys, while bees are groping the roses.
In common knavery, school tapestry, banner-gaudy flaunts
to broadcast her blaze of childhood.
The old da Vinci
tableau perpetuates, down deep aisle shadow, their meal of last resort,
last hope, last moment to record new glints of glory.
From England's oakwood harbour-forgetting, the chancel screen
in intricate bladework, demarcates her prim public
canvas from private holies, where candles
dance their slim knowing, luminous mischief,
flicker-wink and head-nod over
the sacred bed.

Alchemilla and peach roses chorus on dark-gate pew ends.
Deep cut fern fronds wave cool-company damp;
glittering astilbe virgins wait in the wings; flame stock
sweet love-scents
perfume prayer space, dissolving loose lisianthus lips.
Dolphin-dancing delphiniums open flood gates to hot joy.
Hostas harness shade for private
passions in the porch.
Townsfolk all trip through an everlasting, periwinkle trail.
Paradise beckons with children choiring. Little girls
bear up flowers of innocence, from summer's red heat
into the deepening glade; bridesmaids in sage jade
advance the moment's glory of ripening stills.
Same old story makes her wicked entry.
Organ pipes pan-pan the wry, sly god.
Now it begins.

Now, we all know not, under the great green Pentecost blanket
any impediment splashing about
in the still stone, mason-moulded, long Saxon, tick-ticking, clock-
striking,
wild-west-door font,
any reason why God, in his bright northern, heather-

crisp, soon to be purple with passion, high holiday heaven --
and all the deep hot lover mums
flaunting come-get-me
hats – should not sanctify, glorify, celebrate, run riot, grace-grant
inebriate brave blessings on our fabulous unions.
Sermon songs euphemise conjugal fumblings and fancies.
Wear kindness, like a see-through nightie; humility
like goats on a tread-on-me-softly ledge;
gentle patience, forgiveness, compassion.
At our body border, nothing to
declare but love.

We take for wedded husband, wedded wife, to full bed and board;
we have the wildfire and the flood, fair-foul
from this day forward, seedtime, meadowsweet, foxglove and heyday
harvest;
we hold our peace.
According to Goddes holy ordeinance, the hawk
jet flies over the chiming tower, the refugee boat docks
in the river's full, sacred mouth
pouting her kisses.
In sickness, rude health, we hale pigeons for doves on a three-cross
lamp post.
We plight cash in the rat-ditch, skint-in-piper's attic,
pen our own tight dancing rhymes on hassock kneeling cuddles,
sign in the register our secret word, plight our troth.
For better or worse put pen to paper,
harvest daft data sheaves of history
to prove our song in red snatches, till
death us depart.

Under memorial flags of wars, with this ring I thee wed
wrapped in rags, under the vicar's folly
Shadow. With my body I thee worship. Write a new word on red glass.
Let the land expect.
In the name of father, mother, granny and grandad,
billy and sarah, tommy and susan, every last mad jack
in the chatterbox, jill in her
riding night fountain,
saints in hardware, grocer, butcher, angels hymning the sheep-shear
highstreet,

the jubilee hall for a ceilidh, the kiddies' loud
play park, mischief ghosts on the looming sandstone flat table
ice-giant crafted, shafted hills. Let the brown spuggies,
churchmice, beetles, spiders, gay butterflies,
blowflies, dragon flies clap like billyo.
And bright kids write naughty poems
in the register.

Now all year round, the town band plays in the holy, marching
streets.
She, who must forever be adored, looks
over hot bodies. Now all we need is love, while the stone tower bells
ring us bright changes.

Gudbrandsjuvet

We all admire foaming snow in a cauldron,
waterfall miracle, zigzag bridges,
wire and steel sticks, a staircase for salmon
and punnets of blood-red strawberries, sweeter than summer.
But, Gudbrandsjuvet – that takes the biscuit.

I've no problem catching you up in a flash,
leaping with salmon, clearing foam
and all purpose, vaulting memory.
So begin poems. Zigzag, like August whispers,
over the troll-green song, green mountain abyss.

But the man with a camera doubts he took your love
leaping, flew, with you in his arms.
An old, dry, wrinkled man – he'd clearly
forgotten the taste of your kiss on a strawberry,
or how love runs like summer down your chin.

Renaissance

All night, the wind and sea are noisy neighbours,
careless of embarrassment, growling passions,
hard words and tearful endearments. Bodies up-turn
grit sand and moulded stone, on a bone-ridge beach.
Throws of their ecstasy buffet our place by the shore.
Come morning, a curious light, in the eyes of a squall
not yet done, flexing limbs in sycamore
planting, stirs a persistent ruffling of feathers.

Early-day dog-walkers struggle to regain control
of their animal *joie de vivre*. Sky remains grey.
Bluster is never far distant. We are all subject
to sudden drenching, leaving a new-born shining.

The Magnolia Poem

Blousy dancer, scanty clad,
pink as a blush, gauche white,
limp tepals loose,
blow your careless, languid jazz.
Saintly saxophone of sleazy spring,
improvise mid-April blue.

Sent out to hone my skills,
observe, record and analyse,
deep in a lost,
Victorian quarry, where some empire
fire-lord, once, cut his mason stone
to build, amid dark crags, his temple of light.

Weed-wilderness spread vegetable,
urban sprawl. Hogweed riot,
drunken, bramble
trash, nettle sting, erotic
meadowsweet. The willowherb disrobing
shed her spider silks. Hawthorn madness,

briar seduction, bred metamorphic
dancing goddess. Something Sanskrit
in her motion
etched, in sophistries, her morning
ministries, played out in spring science.
All image flickers on a flat, rock wall.

Perplexed by life-cycles, histograms
and youth, I studied quadrat, transect,
sine and slogan,
embroiled in wordy distillations
of the mind until her toxins pricked
my skin, tainted my syllabic organ.

Now, like malaria, symptoms resurface,
directing sacraments, these fifty
years, infecting,
impudent vectors, the last, dividing
cells of an ancient, hoary host,
her long-neglected, fungus-growth of memory.

Fairground Poems

Songs of the carousel, big wheel, swing boat,
helter-skelter, are all I can offer.
Verse from a horde of mirrors,
ghost train rhymes, all I find suitable.
Try-your-strength on a villanelle,
bearded lady sonnet, hook-a-duck limerick.

Circus dregs heap in a trap, strapped
to a flea-yoke harness. Cut them free.
See them fly with the girl on a silver trapeze.
Laugh at them. Weep for them. Ride a mile high with them,
in the clown's mad motorcar. See how they dance
among dodgems, squeal around waltzers,

scorning the safety bar. Loop in octopus
limbs. Fling, centrifugally wide,
a night canto, riding the meteorite.
Cuddle up close, as the slow, green canopy
rises over the caterpillar.
Hear carnival riot under her cover,

spinning your canvas chrysalis moon-wise.
What night moths, painted butterflies,
take form? Head, thorax, abdomen,
dazzling lovers' wings, all wait
their moment perfect. October's antique
mechanical grinds her dark carapace back.

Anthem For The Wingfield Castle

Pre-Humber Bridge, Paddle Steamer, Humber Ferries – Tattershall Castle, Lincoln Castle, Wingfield Castle

Pedalled the arse off those trousers,
    fast as a tabletop layout,
past Saturday matinee pictures (Astoria)
East Park attractions – chain swing, brass slide,
paddling pool and a boat splash to die for.
Second hand shop selling yesterday's frame
all the mad gear for a bad boy's dream.
    Cog-linker, chain-clanker, over the bridge
    that might lift up rivet-eyes, high to the hills,
    to a market place, park-it-place, far away beer
        in the pub, at the station, at pier.

Bought us a ticket for paradise,
    pushed our black-valsparred machines,
like our luck, on the deck of a floating pontoon –
shipful of daredevil, riding astride
green water, like a chuffing goon,
churning the weed in her hair and the mud
a heart-beat drum in country blood.
    Broth-boiling, clay-moiling beater of tides,
    shape-shifter, fog-lifter, out of the sighs,
    bow nudge it, can't budge it boatload of earth,
        capstan's twist of birth.

Litany of gulls was griping.
    Wet wracked wooden timbers
knocked a nautical Morse on the main.
Watched our heart-strand fail in smoke
and sniffed life's barnacle-breath cocaine.
Land unsampled, unexplored,
Venus overboard,
    steam-pumping, pier-jumping master of paddles,
    brass-rodding, wheel-riding, oiler of metals
    over mum Humber's shifting fathoms.
        Boil and beat and rhythm.

Once there, we hit the saddle, humping
    backs down foreign lanes,
over the tide in thorny ways,
father and me. We scanned horizons,

aimed for the red-hot lover's craze.
Found a little england shrinker,
lost our souls to a meddlesome tinker.
    Flood's a border, fence, excursion.
    Glooming fog's a dark diversion.
    Bare the skeleton vision's rattle,
        ragamuffin tittle-tattle.

Way past a forty stop wilderness,
    familiar woods on hand,
now, I bunk with charabancs,
juggernauts and foreign gods,
share a berth with caravans
cabin, class, a tasty diner
on a shoreline wide as China.
    Now, my landscape narrows down
    to margins tight as a nut, or a heart,
    last ferry terminal, pretty fix;
        tuppeny ride on the sticks.

Star Gatherer

Across the moorland moss and stone
she silent stepped her ways alone,
her back was bent and ever still
she pulled the yellow tormentil.
Each atom burst of golden fire
sent shivers through the peat and mire.
Her night was dark. She wandered far,
gleaning a garner full of stars.

For Your Love

I bought you eleven red roses.
You cut their stems,
plunged them into
cheap, clear glass.

Matchstick people
leaning criss-cross
into each other,
green people
kissing
below the meniscus.

Roses

Crimson flower heads,
dark petal edge-waves
dip, curl, mould and cup
bowls and bells, shadow and lip.

Ten days later, still buds bend,
tip spiral in darkness.
Saving destruction,
the centre can never be known.

Deeper line and shape,
each moebius filament cuts down cones.
Sinuous triangle shade and crimson
parchment tissue pinks.

Mind and memory
prime scarlet fever,
while every syllable
aches and shakes and links.

Horse's Joy

Autumn, and a pure white foal
is rolling on rain-soaked grass.
Next field I pass is brown as old dock,
rook-pocked, flapping grey weather rags.
Yellow trees deliver rhyme in billions.
Willowherb scallywags strain to burst their feathers.
Meanwhile, five miles on from horse's joy,
I'm wondering how this world would be,
if unicorns wrote poems.

Pastoral

September poems
fall in a hundred graces,

russet verses,
green as the seven-fingered ash,

golden stanzas
bask in late-flowering sun.

Dark leaves garland you
with woodland singing,

cover your nakedness
with autumn longing.

Marvellust

Had we but world enough and time,
we'd lie in bed till half past nine.
All obstacles to further love
like silk or satin I'd remove but,
as when painting walls and doors
the curves I would caress are yours,
and as my mind in secret lay
most carnally with you all day then,
since we cannot stop the sun,
come love with me till ten past one.

I Am A New Man

Well,
nearly new.

The kind you would find
on trestle tables
in Saturday Methodist,
church hall jumble sales,

next to galleon pots of tea
and bin lid plates of biscuits
with fly currants.
Picked up. Picked over.

Arms held out
to judge the reach.
Rummaged, to see
what's been left in the pockets.

Held up to light
from high windows,
scanning for flaws.
Probably, surreptitiously

sniffed
checking for manliness,
cleanliness (godliness).
Pre-loved. Lifted.

Tried. Tested. Let go.
And all that remains
(after Grandstand)
dumped out back

for the rag and bone cart
of your heart.

Big Liam's Last Poem

Twinkle twinkle little poem
how I wonders where youre goin!
Up above the world so high
symbol, sighman, signify
Tingle tangle little poem
its amazin how youre growin

Pantos Mimos

You were the panto fairy, I was the dame.
All the children laughing was scary.
We were to blame for their wildness, their shrieking
screaming and squeaking, for tears. We were
the fountain of everything, laughter and fear.
You with a wand that fizzed and chortled,
me with a bag and a bust and a dream that sparkled.

There we were, living our fable out
on a stage the world might see. We
had stumbled out of our stable, highly
unsuitable persons for any such drama,
quite unaware we'd unravel former
narrative threads, been set up on boards,
as it were, dancing on air, or the perilous
breath of song.

You with a halo tucked in your belt till you needed it,
me with pink bloomers and leopard-skin tights,
courting the children's approval, delighting in,
feeding it. And of course,
I must warble a cartoon falsetto,
notes unaccustomed. This is not my voice
at all. Yet of course, it has to be. There it is,
whistling out of my head like a prayer,
hope of salvation, or maybe some
half-remembered incantation.

So here we are, haggling over the right
and just, bright in your fairy dust, holding
the stage for an age of starlight, magic and snow.
When all things are possible, credible promises grow.
Up here we make fun, with wild, contorted small faces,
laugh at the dark and an audience yelling
Behind you. Look.
What's behind you?

You'd Think I Was Old Enough To Know Better

More than sixty winters gathering
frost in the north
ought to breed common sense.
Garage roof will leak when ice takes hold,
boiler will lock out.
Candles hide in recalcitrant cupboards.
Torches choose
to leak their terminal waste. Even the prettiest tree
sheds needles over the best-hoovered carpet,
clogging the cleaner.

Spring is all very well, in its place.
Ice-melt tops up
flood potential. Needs
must be wary of torrential giving.
Aggression of snowdrops;
raucous, carnival march of the daffs;
magnolias' naked,
lascivious abandon; savage fecundities
of sheep, and then there's all that
feverish growing.

Summer, of course, is one wild symphony –
much over-rated,
some would say. Strings
too lush; flutes way too flamboyant; oboe
more like a cat
on heat and all those horns! Trumpet
believes he's God.
And tell me, is a trombone supposed to do that? It's all
too much. And the sunburn . . .

Autumn, I suppose, is what
it's all about.
Enjoy the fruits of life
responsibly lived. Ignore the new-term promise
of red ticks.
Settle for conkers at dawn, pipe, slippers and falling
leaves. Bonfires.
A few stray whizz-bangs, tricks
and a harvest of ghosts.

Dead Poet's Poem

The poet was dead,
of that there was never a doubt:
pennies in ears, on eyes and tongue,
brain stuffed tight as a Christmas song
or turkey. Or maybe a cushion,
a thread-bare, tapestry fright –
dead with small change.

Passage was paid
but you came along,
prising up coins till they clinked on the quay,
dropped with a metaphor's plop in the salt
sea and since it was you he detected,
once the silence lifted, his tongue could
do nowt but dance.

What matter the fact
you had no right?
What matter the heart, the hand, the hope,
the dragging, long-shore drift of rope?
What matter the times, by scores,
you stopped his way before?
What matter the failure

of vision? What matter
the endless conversation,
the mindless indecision? What matter
the halting, shapeless, broken rattle?
What matter the tasteless serving,
or the fact his limp, untempered
song was undeserving?

You stepped up,
shook off a skillet full of skins,
dipped your fingers, one last chance,
in a skull, pulled out the plum of a dance,
a lifetime's curious legend,
a dragon-hoard of pigeons,
and flew them home.

Printed in Dunstable, United Kingdom

76514148R00099